Oliver Throck Morton

The Southern Empire, with other Papers

Oliver Throck Morton

The Southern Empire, with other Papers

ISBN/EAN: 9783743309272

Manufactured in Europe, USA, Canada, Australia, Japa

Cover: Foto ©ninafisch / pixelio.de

Manufactured and distributed by brebook publishing software (www.brebook.com)

Oliver Throck Morton

The Southern Empire, with other Papers

CONTENTS.

THE SOUTHERN EMPIRE.

	PAGE
The Conjecture	1
Its Difficulties	2
Presentment of the Federal Grand Jury	3
The Golden Circle	4
The Dream of Empire	4
The Causes of the War as they are writ by its Makers	5
The Slaveholders and the Constitution	6
The Free and Slave Systems briefly compared	8
The Law governing the Economy of the South	9
The Effect of Slavery upon the Slaves, Land, and Agriculture	10
The Planter needed New Soil	11
But he also needed Slaves	12
The Cotton Gin	13
The Cruelties of Slavery	13
The Foreign Slave Trade	14
Governor Adams's Message	15
Other Phases of the Movement	16

CONTENTS.

Extent and Profits of Piratical Slaving	17
International Slave Trade inevitable	17
The Two Objects of Southern Revolution	18
Economics of Slavery further considered	18
Sociology of Slavery	21
Feudalism in the South	21
The "Mean-White" Population	23
The Moral Aspect of Slavery	25
The Politics of Slavery	26
The Gulf of Mexico	27
Florida	28
Destruction of "Negro Fort"	29
Cession of Florida	30
The Second Seminole War	31
The Balance of Power	32
Texas	33
Houston's War	35
Recognition and Annexation of Texas	36
Manifest Destiny	37
Slidell's Mission	37
Contemplated Spoliation and Annexation of Mexico	38
Attitude of the Northern People	39
Compromise of 1850	42
Kansas-Nebraska Bill	43
Benton's Outline of the Southern Empire	43
Gadsden's Mission	44
Cuba	46
Stephen A. Douglas	47
Lopez	48

CONTENTS. vii

Order of the Lone Star	48
Guanajuato	48
Purpose of Southern Secession	51
Crittenden Compromise	52
Thaddeus Stevens	53
The Rebellion the Result of a Conspiracy	53
Provincialism of the Southern People	54
Their Misconception of the North	55
Impotency of the Central Government	56
Bravery of the Southern People in War	58
Disappearance of Republican Forms	59
The Southern Empire	60
Its Military Character	60
Its Growth	61
The Reopening of the Slave Trade	61
Why an Empire and not a Republic	61
Disintegration and Reunion of the North	62
Decline of the Southern Empire	63
Loss of Northern Provinces	64
Suppression of the Slave Trade	64
Fall of the Southern Empire	65

OXFORD.

Introduction	69
Origin of the Town	71
The Castle	71
The Coming of the Monks	72
Alfred not the Founder of the University	73

The Irish Missionaries	73
The Church and Learning	74
The Decline of Learning	75
Charlemagne and Alfred	75
Monastic Instruction	76
Scotus Erigena and Gerbert	77
The Twelfth Century	77
Monastic Schools the Germ Cells of the Universities	78
The Rise of the Halls	78
The Universities as Literary Republics	78
The Term "University"	79
The University of Salernum	79
Saracenic Influence in Europe	80
Irnerius creates the University of Bologna	80
Effect of the Revival of the Roman Law	80
Vacarius in Oxford	81
Conflict between the Civil and the Common Law	81
The "Nations"	82
Migration of Students	84
Two Nations in Oxford	84
Rise of the German University System	85
Secession from Paris	85
Oxford becomes a University	85
Three Secessions from Oxford	86
St. Scholastica's Day	86
The Town does Penance	86
The Number of Students at Oxford	87
Chaucer's Portrait of an Oxford "Clerk"	88
Turbulence of Student Life	89

Advent of the Colleges	89
The University and the Colleges distinct	90
Merton College	90
Balliol College	91
New College	92
Wood's List of Oxford Schoolmen	93
Revival of the Theory of Universals	94
Roscellin and Anselm	94
William of Champeaux and Abelard	94
Hales and Grostête	95
Thomas Aquinas	95
Duns Scotus	96
Ockham ends the Controversy of Universals	96
Ockham the Forerunner of Wycliffe	97
Failure of the Scholastic System	98
Meagreness of Knowledge	99
Roger Bacon	101
Physical Attributes of Mediæval Oxford	103
Pestilence at Oxford	104
The Art of Medicine	105
Wycliffe	106
Jesus College	108
The Beginnings of English Prose	109
Tyndale and Campanella	110
Colet, More, and Erasmus	111
Oxford in Advance of Wittenberg	113
"Greeks and Trojans" at Oxford	114
Bruno visits Oxford	115
The Heliocentric Doctrine	116

Religious Persecution at Oxford	116
Under Henry VIII.	116
Under Edward VI.	117
Under Mary	118
Ridley, Latimer, and Cranmer	118
Bodleian Library	119
Leicester's Work as Chancellor . . .	119
Amy Robsart	120
Her Funeral	120
Mistakes of Scott	121
St. Mary the Virgin's Church	122
Magdalen College	122
Its Gardens	122
Addison	123
Vandalism of the Puritans . .	123
King Charles in the Town	124
Cromwell as Chancellor	124
Song of "The English Anacreon" . . .	125
University Decree of 1683	128
James II. in Oxford	129
William Penn expelled from Christ Church . .	130
Origin of Christ Church	130
Its Bells	131
Expulsion of John Locke . . .	132
John Wesley at Oxford	133
The Methodist Club	133
Whitefield	133
Wesley's Political Sermon	134
His Epitaph	134

Berkeley and Butler	135
Tractarianism	135
Gibbon expelled from Magdalen	137
Doctor Johnson of Pembroke	137
Shelley and Landor expelled	137
The University of the Last Century	138
The Modern University	139
Oxford and Cambridge	140

SOME POPULAR OBJECTIONS TO CIVIL SERVICE REFORM.

Do Revolutions go backwards?	145
Introduction of the Spoils System	146
Andrew Jackson	147
Theory of the American Commonwealth	148
Madison's Theory of Removal	148
Political Brigandage	149
The Reformers	150
The Civil Service Law	150
First Forty Years of the Republic	151
Feudal System in American Politics	153
The Spoils System and the Slave System	154
Doctrine of Civil Service Reform	158
The President and the Clerk	163
Anglophobia	166
The Spoils System imported from England	167
Civil Service Reform in England	168
Aristocracy	171

Bureaucracy	172
Insolence of Office	172
The Professional Politician	173
His Absolute Power	174
The Citizen as an Office-Holder	175
The Office-Holder in Politics	177
Competitive Examinations	178
Their Educational Value	180
Their Influence upon Character	181
Qualifications of the Office-Holder	182
Functions of the Commission	183
Impotency of Heads of Bureaus	184
Jackson and the Four-Year Law	185
Corruption of Jackson's Administration	186
Deficits under Van Buren	187
Rotation in Office	187
Its Possibilities	188
Business and Politics	189
The Art of Administration in the United States	190
Incapacity of Municipal Government	190
Presidential Appointments	191
The Cabinet	192
Rotation in the United States	193
View of the Founders of the Republic	194
Change wrought by Custom	196
Calhoun on the Four-Year Law	197
Theory of John Stuart Mill	198
Election of Postmasters	199
Responsibility Vital to Good Government	200

Weakness of the Four-Year Law	201
The Act of 1820	202
Later Legislation	203
Limited Application of the Pendleton Act	204
The Four-Year Law should be repealed	205
Effects of Rotation summarized	206

THE SOUTHERN EMPIRE.

THE SOUTHERN EMPIRE.[1]

WHAT would be the condition of the Western world to-day if Southern rebellion had become revolution? is a question which may sometimes give us pause.

Unfortunately, it is growing increasingly difficult to answer it; to realize the past, and thereby to imagine what would have been. The war has nearly lapsed from memory into tradition. Its triumphs and sufferings, its hopes and fears, are fast fading with distance, and soon will be wrapped in the mists of forgetfulness. The imagination, dulled by time, fails longer to body forth the forms of averted perils, and the dread alternative, disunion, has almost lost its meaning. Yet it was once real enough, near enough.

[1] The economic and historic data contained in this essay are drawn from sources easily accessible, and will be readily identified by the good readers of history. Marginal references are, therefore, omitted.

In the downfall of the slave power a distinct civilization perished, with institutions and ideals alien to the age; and "the next generation [says a recent biographer of Calhoun] will find it easier to form an adequate conception of the ancient Egyptians and Indians than of their own grandfathers." The historian with much to record concerns himself but little with a contingency which did not occur, and the probable future of the great slave federation barely receives from him the empty compliment of a passing conjecture. The difficulties in the way of a philosophical forecast may be pleaded in extenuation, for they are great. But if there be a science of history based upon a study of uniformities, if we may reason from cause to effect in human affairs, deducing the laws which govern a certain state of society, and, *per contra*, deducing a civilization from the continued operation of certain laws, the social and economic conditions existing in the South before the war are a legitimate subject of investigation, and furnish a basis for rational speculation. What is, we know; what was to have been, let us consider.

During the May term, 1862, the Federal grand jury for the District of Indiana returned nearly two hundred indictments of persons belonging to a certain treasonable organization, known as the Knights of the Golden Circle, — a society formed to discourage enlistments in the Union armies, and otherwise to give aid and comfort to the States then in rebellion. At the conclusion of its labors, the grand jury made a presentment to the court, which contained the following paragraph : —

"From the evidence introduced before said grand jury, it would seem that the Order called the Knights of the Golden Circle had its origin in some of the Southern States, and was introduced into this State from Kentucky. Its primary object, when it originated, was to organize the friends of the institution of African slavery in the United States for the purpose of acquiring more territory in Mexico and the Central American States ; also the acquisition of Cuba, thereby to extend and foster a great slave empire, even though it should dye those countries in human blood. Hence the various raids made upon those countries."

These conclusions are the gleanings of an

examination of many witnesses made by a jury possessing character and intelligence, and are significant as affording not merely a key to the purposes of a secret order, but a revelation of the real aim and object of the great slave movement itself. Whatever the extent and importance of the Knights of the Golden Circle, that society was, in its essence, truly representative of the daring ambition of the Southern leaders. Its purpose was, as has been stated, to found a gigantic tropical slave empire. The Golden Circle was a line drawn from Havana as a centre, with a radius of sixteen degrees latitude and longitude. Here was a vast domain adapted to slave labor, extending from the confluence of the Ohio and the Mississippi to the Isthmus of Darien, and from the West Indies to the Pacific coast of Mexico.

Mr. Draper, the historian, in his composite of Southern opinion, pictures this imperial realm:

"As the Romans, basing their political life on a slave system, and availing themselves of the advantages of an interior sea, soon brought their feebler neighbors into subjection, solidly establishing themselves all around the Mediterranean, so the Gulf of

Mexico and the Caribbean will be a Mediterranean for us. Feeble communities, such as those of Mexico and Central America, can be easily conquered by arms, or still more easily by gold. They will submit to the fate of Egypt, and Syria, and Greece. Cuba, Jamaica, Hayti will follow the fate of Cyprus, Sardinia, Sicily. Across a narrow isthmus is the Pacific Ocean, and where the West merges into the East are the venerable empires and the wealth of Asia."

Such the dream! Truly, a regal concept of barbaric splendor, as alluring to the adventurous as the cloud-built city of the Sun, which sits enthroned at the horizon, a gleaming cluster of golden minarets and spires. Was it as insubstantial? Was it but the despairing hope of the fatuous, the idle fantasy of the fool? Let us see.

The secret history of the war remains to be written, the motives of the leading conspirators to be explored. The alleged causes of the conflict from the pens of some of them, the enumeration of constitutional quibbles, are mere casuistry. The President and the Vice-President of the Southern Confederacy would have a credulous posterity believe that the South tried to separate from the North, at the expense of a bloody and desolating war, simply to establish a naked and abstract proposition of constitutional law. But posthumous confessions, offered by way of special pleading, are not the sole repositories of history. It is writ otherwise, unconsciously yet indelibly. The slaveholders in the pursuit of their ends were utterly indifferent to constitutional trammels. They used the Constitution as a shield or a sword, as necessity or convenience dictated. They adopted what has been called the "patent reversible process of construction." They localized slavery in the Territories of Missouri, Arkansas, and Florida by loose construction, and when those Territories became States they protected it from governmental interference by strict construction. When they agreed to the Missouri Compromise, which prohibited slavery in all of the territory north of line 36° 30′, they affirmed the power of Congress to regulate slavery in the Territories. Afterwards, when they failed to extend this line through the Mexican purchase, they repealed the Missouri Compromise, and advocated the doctrine of squatter sovereignty, namely, that the people of the Territories must decide the question of slavery for themselves, free from congressional interference and without reference to latitude. But in the struggle to make the free soil of Kansas slave, they were unsuccessful, and then came the Dred Scott decision, which overturned both of the preceding propositions by denying in effect the power either of the people or of Congress to keep slavery out of any Territory. The conflict which followed was "irrepressible." Mr. Calhoun and the abolitionists were the prophets of their time. Had there been no doctrine of state sovereignty, the exigencies of slavery would have devised it; or, even lacking it, the South would have justified its action in the residuary right of revolution, should it have cared to justify it at all. As a matter of fact, at the time of secession, "a decent respect to the opinions of mankind" did not, in its judgment, require that it should declare the causes which impelled the separation. We may, therefore, in this brief review, skirt the howling deserts of constitutional law, and seek a more fruitful region.

II.

To the American of the commercial present the scheme of empire above adverted to may seem to be highly visionary. The dry recital of the American court reads like a page of romance, fictious and fanciful. Yet it contains the soberest fact in American history. The Knights of the Golden Circle and the Order of the Lone Star, together with the countless other filibustering societies which abounded in the South during forty years before the war, were but the natural expression of the tendencies of the slave system. They were the symptoms of a disease, the evidence of a state of mind.

Fundamentally, the rebellion was a contest between two antagonistic labor or social systems, the one free, the other slave; the one industrial and based upon contract, the other militant and based upon status. The one encouraged individual independence, promoted intelligence, and fostered invention, thereby multiplying its productive power many fold; the other crushed the spirit by fettering the body, and conserved ignorance. The one invited immigration by ennobling labor; the other repelled immigration by making labor the badge of servitude. The one created citizens, the other subjects. In fine, the one tended to build up a free republic, the other tended to the construction of a servile empire.

The unwritten, irreversible law governing the economy of the South demanded two things: a progressively expanding territory and an increase in the number of slaves. As these were the organic forces which made for empire, they require a somewhat extended and technical exposition.

The acquisition of land by the South was an economical necessity. Slave labor impoverished and tainted where it touched. It was "unskillful and given reluctantly." The slave worked just enough to avoid corporal or other punishment, as the value of any superior degree of efficiency accrued to the master and not to himself. Increased zeal meant increased burden. Slaves must be watched, and therefore, working in gangs, their usefulness was curtailed. They were confined to the culture of cotton, tobacco, sugar, and rice, which admitted of the employment of many within a limited space, under the eye of the overseer. But on cereal lands they could not be maintained except at a loss. One freeman for several acres of wheat, and several slaves for one acre of cotton, roughly defines the limitations of the slave system. The slaves lacked versatility. They were unfitted for manufacturing, as they had not the deftness and education essential to the artisan, nor the stimulation of material gain or of prospective emancipation. Instructed with difficulty in the art of growing one staple, they could not readily be transferred to the culture of another, and the rotation of crops thus became an impossibility. Nor could the planter let his fields lie fallow. The support of his slaves was a constant drain upon his resources, and enforced a continuous tillage that met with a steadily diminishing return. Moreover, with his entire capital invested in slaves, the planter had nothing to apply to the improvement of his lands. Even were it possible, it were useless, to purchase agricultural implements of improved construction, as they could not be intrusted to the care of slaves.

Looked at in any way, agriculture, under the Southern system, was, and must have been, "artless and exhausting." The barren tobacco lands of Virginia and the Carolinas, and the abandoned plantations throughout the South, eloquently bespoke this fact. The planter needed virgin soil obtainable at a nominal price; he would have it. This, then, was one object to be attained by revolution. But, it may be urged, that at the time of secession, only a small portion of the land of the South was under cultivation; that political representation had been the sole object of the aggressions of the slave power; and that the greed for land would cease with the South's connection with the Union. It is sufficient to reply that, so crude were the processes of slave labor, none but the choicest lands, those teeming with fertility, could be cultivated profitably, and these conditions imply comparative scarcity. Inferior soils, which an enlightened free labor could have made richly productive, and which in a free country would have been resorted to under pressure of population, were of necessity neglected as wastes, so that the disproportion mentioned was more apparent than real. If in 1860 the planter did not need more land for the purposes of cultivation, he would need it within a proximate period, and he must hold the right secure to obtain such land by any means that he might see fit, be they fair or foul. The Northern conscience was an embarrassing trammel, and might not accommodate itself readily to the requirements of the slave system. Restrict slavery to definite limits, and it must inevitably perish. A redundant population cannot subsist upon an exhausted-soil. Imprisonment meant death. The planter saw this clearly, and when he received his first decisive check in the Kansas-Nebraska struggle, he threw down the gage of battle, and raised the banner of Empire.

But there was a more pressing need than land — slaves. Although a clause denouncing slavery had been stricken from the Declaration of Independence, at the instance of South Carolina and Georgia, it was expected, at the time of the adoption of the Constitution, that slavery would soon die out of itself. Indeed, the Constitution contemplated the abolition of the slave trade in 1808, and when that year came, the protest of the slaveholders was of the feeblest. But with the invention of the cotton gin there was a permanent revival of slavery. When the planters realized that a negro, with the aid of this machine, could cleanse three hundred and fifty pounds of cotton in a day, whereas, formerly, without it, he could cleanse only a few pounds, the price of slaves rose enormously, and the South had found a product which, it thought, would command the wealth, and rule the markets of the civilized world. As the production of cotton increased, the relations of master and slave lost "whatever patriarchal character they possessed," with the exception of the household slaves, who were generally well treated, and slavery became "a heartless business speculation." The life of a slave was estimated in so many bales of cotton. Owing to the cruelty and the excessive burdens imposed, the time of the effective labor of a slave on the cotton plantations was reduced to seven years, and on the sugar plantations to five years. This process, together with the exhaustion of the soil, was pushing the color line farther south, year by year. The price of slaves was rising rapidly. The reopening of the slave trade was a necessity and must precede territorial extension. A Georgian delegate to the Charleston convention in 1860 went to the root of the matter when he said: —

"I believe that this doctrine of protection to slavery in the Territories is a mere theory, a mere abstraction. Practically, it can be of no consequence to the South, for the reason that the infant has been strangled before it was born. You have cut off the supply of slaves; you have crippled the institution in the States by your unjust laws, and it is mere folly and madness now to ask protection for a nonentity, for a thing which is not there. We have no slaves to carry to those Territories. We can never make another slave State with our present supply of slaves. And if we could, it would not be wise, for the reason that if you make another slave State from your new Territories with the present supply of slaves, you will be obliged to give another State — either Maryland, Delaware, or Virginia — to free soil upon the North."

But Virginia, a slave market, was opposed to competition; and the Georgian retorted: —

"It has been my fortune to go into that noble old State to buy a few darkies, and I have had to pay from $1,000 to $2,000 a head, when I could go to Africa and buy better negroes at $50 apiece. Unquestionably it is to the interest of Virginia to break down the African slave trade, when she can sell her negroes at $2,000."

The Georgian delegate was by no means singular in his views. The foreign and domestic slave trade might differ from each other in degree, perhaps, but not in kind; and an objection which would lie against the one, and not against the other, must be sentimental rather than practical. This, at least, was the view of many planters and politicians of the South. The prohibition of the slave trade was felt to be a brand upon the slaveholder. In a message to the Legislature of South Carolina (1857), Governor Adams argued that "if the slave trade be piracy, the slave must be plunder;" and he urged the withdrawal of "assent to an act which is in itself a direct condemnation of your institutions." In 1858, a bill authorizing a company to import twenty-five hundred African negroes, who were to be indentured for at least fifteen years, passed the Louisiana House of Representatives, and failed by only two votes in the Senate. To offer a premium for the best specimen of an imported African and to propose a prize for the best sermon upon the ethics of such an importation were but incidents of the movement. Jefferson Davis saw "no inhumanity or sinfulness" in the slave trade, while Alexander H. Stephens wished to impress upon the Southern mind "the great truth that without an increase of African slaves from abroad" many more slave States need not be looked for.

However, the South determined to bide the issue of the war before attempting to force the question. The constitutional prohibition of the slave trade, adopted at Montgomery, was a part of the price of Virginia's withdrawal from the Union, and was a concession to the sentiment of Europe, whose sympathy and aid the South needed and expected. The slave trade was only a question of time; it would "bring slaves to the poor man, increase the population, and thereby the value of land." Legal enactments prohibiting it would be inoperative, and as a matter of fact they were. It is estimated that, during eighteen months of 1859 and 1860, eighty-five vessels were fitted out from New York city alone for the slave trade, and that from thirty to sixty thousand negroes were brought to the United States annually. De Bow's Commercial Review calculated in 1857 that forty slavers were making a net annual profit of about seventeen millions of dollars. It is certain that, under the Confederate government, the provision prohibiting the slave trade would have broken down utterly, were it not formally stricken out of the Constitution. The demand for cotton, which, judged from the past, would increase at the rate of nearly 100 per cent. in a decade, would make this imperative, because the production of slaves could not be expected to increase more than thirty per cent. in the same period. Thus the reopening of the slave trade was the second object to be attained by revolution.

But more land meant the conquest of Mexico and Central America, as physical and political conditions were a sufficient bar to a northerly or westerly extension of the Southern system; and more slaves meant the annexation of Cuba,—a slave nursery,—and renewed commerce with the distant coasts of Africa. The inexorable logic of successful rebellion was the creation of a tropical slave empire.

III.

That this empire was the inevitable product of natural and social laws is a proposition susceptible of much illustration. Slavery was the basal fact of Southern society, the corner-stone of a feudal superstructure. An impoverished people can be neither independent nor intellectual, and slavery was bankrupting the South. It not only exaggerated the natural inequalities of the distribution of wealth, — that primal cause of the world's social disorders, — it paralyzed production. Itself inefficient, it encouraged improvidence. The planters were heavily in debt to Northern capitalists, no less because of the wastefulness of the slave system and the abnormally large amount of capital that it required, than because of their own extravagance. Where to labor is ignominy, prudence, economy, and careful business methods fall under the ban. The great wealth of the South was a delusion. The Northern hay crop alone exceeded in value that of the Southern cotton, tobacco, and rice crops. Cotton was king by usurpation, not by right. The forcing system reduced the price, and narrowed the margin of profit to the vanishing point. But the price of slaves suffered no reduction, being governed by the market value in the most productive regions. The number of plantations decreased, the larger absorbing the smaller. There was little diversity of industry in the South, "slave agriculture by a sure law banishing all pursuits but its own." The South was an exporter of raw materials, and an importer of almost all finished fabrics, necessaries as well as luxuries. The slave system forbade immigration, and the South lost heavily by emigration. More than a half million of its citizens sought the Middle and Western States, carrying with them prejudices, which afterwards found expression in the black laws, and in active sympathy with Southern and Northwestern secession. Capital was also driven to the North, seeking profitable investment. In the sectional rivalry slavery made but a halting race. The great natural resources of the South, the exuberant fertility of the soil, the richness of the mineral deposits, and the commercial advantages afforded by the coast line and by the great rivers, availed it naught. At the beginning of government, North and South were nearly equal in population, trade, and property. But within seventy years, the disproportion between the numbers and the wealth of the two sections became very great and striking, and was clearly traceable to the economic systems respectively existing. Out of these systems grew two civilizations, which, differing in fundamentals, were at last formally arrayed against each other. That of the North was instinct with life and progress; that of the South was a relic of the dark ages. The one was the rosy child of the dawn; the other, the gruesome spectre of a departing night.

The South was never a republic in the Northern or democratic sense of the word. It was government by aristocracy. Its civilization partook somewhat of the Middle Ages, in that the redress of many wrongs was referred to the arbitrament of arms, and in that the laws, as in the dawn of European jurisprudence, were useful in confirming the abuses of a social system. There were few large towns, and the planters lived apart upon their estates, like the feudal lords of an agricultural community before the rise of manufacturing. They were the owners of the soil which was cultivated by their serfs. Their allegiance to the central government they held as lightly as ever did feudal chief hold his allegiance to the crown, and finally they took up arms against it. The Barons' wars may be found in miniature in the Southern feuds, whereby whole families were sometimes extirpated. In the arts of social life the resemblance was strong. The planters, a leisure class, lived a free and open-handed life. They devoted themselves to excitement and pleasure, and these they found in pursuits as diverse as politics, gambling, and field sports. A constant contact with a degrading servitude made them intensely jealous of their superiority and liberties, while their absolutism was that of the manorial lord. They were brave to daring, high spirited, arrogant, and brutal in controversy; and they gloried in a bastard chivalry. They accepted slavery as an ordinance of nature, and they adopted its cruelties without mitigating them. But to say that the slaveholders were nevertheless distinguished by undeniable virtues is to utter no greater paradox than is to be found upon every page of the history of morals. They were in, but not of, the industrial age, and they possessed the vices and virtues of their stage of civilization. Among their finer attributes was a genial and florid hospitality, which was partly the outgrowth of the loneliness of plantation life. The social atmosphere of the South possessed a certain indolent charm imparted to it by a leisure class who were also dominant. There was an absence of the compelling rigors of the Northern climate, and of the Puritanic element which takes the world and its work seriously. Outside the planter aristocracy, the South was poor in all that goes to make up modern civilized life. Slavery bore upon it with the weight of a dead hand. Science was without place where society was in a primitive state, and useless where labor was degraded. The diffusion of population acted as a bar to the growth of the professions, and to systematic instruction. Education was denied by legal sanction to one third of the population, and like law, was the patrimony of the rich. But the sociological condition of the South was most vividly reflected in that melancholy product of the slave system, the vagrant or "mean-white" population. In a slave country there is no place for the *bourgeoisie*, the well-to-do middle class, who, in Europe, have served as the bulwark of liberty. As the shortest way to a proper understanding of the social effect of slave labor, I may be pardoned a long quotation from a work of an eminent political economist, the late Mr. Cairnes. He says: —

"It happens that there are in all slave countries vast districts, becoming, under the deteriorating effects of slave industry, constantly larger, which are wholly surrendered to nature and remain forever as wilderness. This is a characteristic feature in the political economy of the Slave States of the South, and is attended with social consequences of the most important kind. For the tracts thus left, or made desolate, become in time the resort of a numerous horde of people, who, too poor to keep slaves and too proud to work, prefer a vagrant and precarious life spent in the desert to engaging in occupations which would associate them with the slaves whom they despise. In the Southern States no less than five millions of human beings[1] are now said to exist in this manner in a condition little removed from savage life, eking out a wretched subsistence by hunting, by fishing, by hiring themselves out for occasional jobs, by plunder. Combining the restlessness and contempt for regular industry peculiar to the savage with the vices of the *prolétaire* of civilized communities, these people make up a class at once degraded and dangerous, and, constantly reinforced as they are by all that is idle, worthless, and lawless among the population of the neighboring States, form an inexhaustible preserve of ruffianism, ready at hand for all the worst purposes of Southern ambition. The planters complain of these people for their idleness, for corrupting their slaves, for their thievish propensities; but they cannot dispense with them; for in truth they perform an indispensable function in the economy of slave societies, of which they are at once the victims and the principal supports. It is from their ranks that those filibustering expeditions are recruited, which have been found so effective an instrument in extending the domain of the slave power; they fur-

---

[1] This number is undoubtedly exaggerated.

nish the border ruffians who, in the colonization struggle with the Northern States, contend with Free-soilers in the Territories, and it is to their antipathy to the negroes that the planters securely trust for repressing every attempt at servile insurrection. Such are the 'mean whites' or 'white trash' of the Southern States. They comprise several local subdivisions, the 'crackers,' the 'sand-hillers,' the 'clay-eaters,' and many more. The class is not peculiar to any one locality, but is the invariable outgrowth of negro slavery wherever it has raised its head in modern times. It may be seen in the new State of Texas, as well as in the old settled districts of Virginia, the Carolinas, and Georgia; in the West India Islands no less than on the Continent." [1]

As the slave system of the Roman Republic created vast landed estates in Italy, and drove the free laborers to the cities, where, fed upon public largesses, voted by ambitious demagogues, they made a despotic empire the alternative of anarchy, so the slave system of the South sapped the vitality of free government by

[1] *The Slave Power*, J. E. Cairnes, pp. 54, 55. New York, 1861. A remarkable book, now out of print. Reviewed by John Stuart Mill, *Diss. and Diss.*, vol. iii. p. 264.

making homeless outcasts of American citizens, and by creating a plutocracy.

Of the moral aspect of slavery it is unnecessary to speak at length. A system which gave repute to slave breeding it is not difficult to characterize. Even the church was summoned to the defense of an institution which violated those great primary laws that we justly hold divine, — the right of human freedom and the sanctity of wifehood. Slavery tore families asunder at the auction block, and sold the members to a living death. It made marriage vows as false as dicers' oaths, and sweet religion a rhapsody of words. Fortified in selfish greed, it enlisted to its support the lowest instincts of man, and transfigured with hate the face of mercy. It corrupted the master, the slave, and the circumjacent community.

IV.

So much for the tendencies of the slave system. Turning now to something more tangible, to those pages of history which record the supremacy of the slave power, we shall find our deduction verified by an ample induction. With the purchase of Florida, the slave interest, just then crystallizing into that aggressive, unscrupulous, and despotic oligarchy, the slave power, entered upon its career of stupendous conquest, which was so nearly to end in the creation of a gigantic tropical slave empire. The attempts, unsuccessful and otherwise, made by the slaveholders to acquire Florida, Texas, California, Mexico, Cuba, and Central America are but the successive steps of an evolution proceeding along the lines of economic law. The end to be attained, however romantic and daring it may seem to be to us, was entirely practical, and only a frightful civil war served to defeat it. Southward the course of empire held its way.

From the time of Cortes the country encompassing the Gulf of Mexico and the Caribbean had dazzled the imagination of adventurers, and had tempted many of them to their death. The mysteries of its shores were celebrated by the wonder loving. There swooned the air, heavy with fragrance; the embracing skies were liquid depths of azure. Nature was rich in color, and was adorned with precious gems, which awaken in tremulous beauty to the kiss of the light. In the forest aisles the music of birds mingled with the sweet chimings of the waters of the fountain of eternal youth, and near by lay hidden the golden city, the very Eldorado of song and story. It was dreamland. After the colonies had achieved independence, this region attracted the attention of statesmen. Hamilton, who had his eye upon Florida, encouraged Miranda in his filibustering expeditions against the Spanish-American possessions, Jefferson bought Louisiana, and Burr undertook his futile venture against Mexico.

It has been said that there were utilitarian reasons entirely apart from the interests of slavery which demanded the cession of Florida. This is true of the taking of West Florida. But in the acquisition of the peninsula slavery was an efficient agent. Of the resources of East Florida, next to nothing was known. Generally, that province was regarded as a huge wilderness and swamp, and was chiefly desirable because it afforded a refuge for fugitive slaves beyond the jurisdiction of the United States. The history of the acquisition is long and scandalous, and need not be told here. It is a story of desultory warfare, ofttimes merciless, against whomsoever should harbor fugitive slaves, or should otherwise harass the Georgian frontier, be the offenders Creeks, Seminoles, or Spaniards. It involved gross treachery, murder, and wanton invasion of foreign soil. Five times in seven years was Florida invaded: once during the war of 1812, by General Jackson, and twice during the same period by Georgia's lawless expeditions. To Georgia, a State which had been largely instrumental in forcing the three fifths provision upon the Constitutional Convention, in securing a twenty years' lease of legal life to the slave trade, and in debasing the first exercise of the national treaty-making power to the return of her fugitive slaves, belongs the invidious distinction of first harnessing the filibusters to the slave car. After the war of 1812, the United States disavowed Georgia's arbitrary invasions, and Florida was reluctantly abandoned. Temporarily, however. A fort on the Appalachicola River,—sixty miles beyond the boundary of the United States,—which had been seized as a defensive post by the Florida exiles, appeared to the Georgian mind to be a constant menace to the repose of a slave society, and General Jackson ordered it to be destroyed. A red-hot shot from a United States gunboat exploded the magazine of the fort, thereby instantly killing two hundred and seventy of the occupants (two thirds of whom were women and children), and wounding all but three of the rest. Those negroes who recovered from their wounds were restored to Georgian claimants, being given up in some instances, we are told, "to the descendants of those who claimed to have owned their ancestors generations before." Twenty years later, Congress suitably rewarded this gallant deed with an appropriation.

The fifth and last invasion of Florida was made by Jackson under cover of the first Seminole war, which was a heritage of the slaughter at "Negro Fort." Jackson promised the President that he would conquer Florida within sixty days, and his was no idle word. An observance of the niceties of international law, as well as of the rules of civilized warfare, did not distinguish this raid of conquest from other undertakings of a similar character. The aid of diplomacy had been invoked long before, and Spain, powerless to protect her citizens and territory from outrage, now agreed to sell Florida. Of one condition, however, she was tenacious to the end, — the United States must abandon all claims to Texas. As the slaveholders were eager, Texas was signed away. It would doubtless be recovered in good time when it was needed. Thus, in short, were seventy-nine thousand square miles of territory gained for slavery. If the purpose of this purchase was to quiet the border, the treaty signally failed. The negroes continued to seek asylum among the Seminoles, and the government decreed the banishment of that tribe to the West, together with the subjection of it to the Creek Indians, who claimed the Seminole exiles as their slaves.

Out of this unfortunate order grew that bloody, protracted, and expensive man-hunt known as the second Seminole war. Among the collateral causes of this war may be mentioned the application of the rule, *partus sequitur ventrem*, to the children of those Indians who had married slave women. Under cover of this law, the half-breed wife of Osceola, a Seminole chief, was seized while she was visiting Fort King. Her husband took a stealthy and terrible revenge; and this was the beginning of general hostilities. Afterwards Osceola himself was taken by treachery, and died in prison. But indeed the whole conflict was marked with great perfidy and cruelty. For the purpose of tracking the slave exiles, the legislature of Florida authorized the purchase of Cuban bloodhounds, and, as an incentive to his soldiers, General Jesup offered captive negroes as prizes of war. The struggle lasted six years, and resulted in reclaiming to slavery five hundred fugitives, at a cost to the United States of $80,000 for each person reënslaved.

V.

The enterprise to which the slaveholders next directed their energies was nothing less than the stealing of an empire. In the lower house of Congress the slave States were in a hopeless minority, although their representation there was based partly upon an enumeration of slaves. To preserve an equality in the Senate, where the representation was arbitrary, was therefore indispensable. A slave State must be found as a complement to every new free State admitted. But the slave power could look only to the Southwest for new States, and there an event had occurred which threatened to close to them forever this highway to future dominion.

In 1821, revolution had swept away the authority of Spain in North America, and Texas-Coahuila became a member of the new State of Mexico, under a constitution which made freedom a birthright, and which forbade the importation of slaves. In 1829, the dictator of Mexico, Guerrero, freed all persons held in slavery within his dominions, and this decree was reaffirmed afterwards in the constitutions of the Mexican republic. The American slave power hastened to meet the impending danger. Texas must be recovered at all hazards, and speedily. The refusal of the Mexican government to entertain any proposition of purchase cut off the only means of lawful acquisition, and thereupon Texas became the subject of a far-reaching intrigue. The Southwest had never been reconciled to the cession of Texas, and individuals anticipated, in a measure, the after-designs of the slave power by undertaking to colonize this territory for their own gain and profit. Only a few months subsequent to the making of the Florida treaty, Long, at the head of a band of Mississippi filibusters, entered Texas, and proclaimed its independence. There being as yet no settlers from the United States in Texas, the project failed. Later, adventurers from Tennessee, Mississippi, and Louisiana went to Texas under the guise of persecuted Roman Catholics, and obtained grants of land from Mexico, which was a Catholic state. These pious gentlemen offered land premiums for the importation of slaves, and opened up a lucrative trade which extended even to Africa. Swindling land companies were organized, and worthless stock and scrip, purporting to be preparatory titles to land, were floated in large quantities. By means such as these, many Northern people became financially interested in the annexation of the new State. Slaves were introduced into Texas from the United States in open defiance of law, or under the technical description of "apprentices for ninety-nine years," and Mexican laws limiting apprenticeship to ten years, and totally prohibiting immigration from the United States, became dead letters when the troops sent to enforce them were recalled to the capital. The time was now ripe actively to assist emigration to Texas, and the slave power set rolling thither "the tide of vagrant blackguardism." "There was probably never seen a more ferocious company of ruffians than Texas contains at this moment," wrote Harriet Martineau in 1835. Arms and stores were sent to them as sinews for the coming war. General Sam Houston, an intimate friend of President Jackson, who himself had vainly endeavored to purchase Texas, went to that province with the avowed intention of wresting it from Mexico. With the details of the contest which followed we are not concerned. The complete success achieved by Houston is a matter of history. It is of more moment to observe that slavery was made the corner-stone of the new Texan republic, and that the Constitution of that State denied the power of emancipation to its Congress, or to any slaveholder, unless he had the consent of Congress. This instrument was adopted in March, 1836, and the recognition of Texas by the United States followed promptly at the next session of Congress. Texas being independent, its annexation to the American Union was a foregone conclusion. England, a heavy creditor to the new State, might foreclose upon the government itself, and abolish slavery, thus making Houston's war nugatory. And there were other contingencies. The slave power of the United States endeavored during ten years to obtain the two thirds vote in the Senate necessary to the ratification of an annexation treaty, and finally, despairing of it, it annexed Texas by joint resolution. As the independence of Texas had not yet been conceded by Mexico, annexation was a *casus belli*. Even this offense our weaker neighbor seemed willing to condone, and diplomacy might have averted bloody strife; but the slaveholders would not have it so. Their appetite had grown by what it fed upon, and they demanded more land. The Rio Grande, and not the Nueces River, said they, was the western boundary of Texas, and thus was the United States embarked upon another unholy war of conquest. This struggle, like the war of 1812, was fomented by the South under cover of "manifest destiny." To Young Democracy, the second conflict with Great Britain meant not only protection, but vindication. They had in view the conquest of Canada. Nay, even more. John Randolph, who satirized the dream of the visionaries, "seemed to see the capital in motion towards the falls of the Ohio, after a short sojourn taking its flight to the Mississippi, and finally alighting at Darien, which . . . will be a most eligible seat of government for the new republic (or empire) of the two Americas." Truth is stranger than fiction, and these words read like a shrill prophecy. Events followed fast in the direction pointed out by the cynic of Roanoke. The cession of New Mexico and California to the United States at the treaty of Guadaloupe Hidalgo was no afterthought. The ambition of the slaveholders was not confined to the territory between the Rio Grande and the Nueces. Before the beginning of hostilities, Slidell had been sent to Mexico to offer $25,000,000 for New Mexico and California, provinces which afterward cost us $95,000,000, not to mention 30,000 lives.

VI.

The underlying purpose of the Mexican war was brought to view as early as 1842, when Henry A. Wise (whose intrigues afterwards made Calhoun Secretary of State) "babbled the whole project" (to use the words of John Quincy Adams) in a speech delivered in the House of Representatives:—

"Let her [Texas] once raise the flag of foreign conquest, let her once proclaim a crusade against the rich States south of her . . . [and] volunteers from all the States in the great valley of the Mississippi, before whom no Mexican troops could stand an hour, would plant the lone star of the Texas banner upon the Mexican capital. They would drive Santa Anna to the south, and the boundless wealth of captured towns and rifled churches, and a lazy, vicious, and luxurious priesthood would soon enable Texas to pay her soldiers and redeem her state debt, and push her victorious arms to the very shores of the Pacific. And would not all this extend slavery? Yes, slavery should pour itself abroad without restraint, and find no limit but the Southern Ocean."

This impetuous utterance affords a picture of what probably would have happened had the slave power been unbridled. As it was, the slave party went far. At the conclusion of the Mexican war, wholesale annexation was openly advocated by Democratic meetings, and by leading journals throughout the United States, and President Polk gave this feeling articulate expression, by declaring in his annual message to Congress : —

" If, after affording this encouragement and protection, and after all the persevering and sincere efforts we have made from the moment Mexico commenced the war [sic], and prior to that time, to adjust our differences with her, we shall ultimately fail, then we shall have exhausted all honorable means in pursuit of peace, and must continue to occupy her country with our troops, taking the full measure of indemnity into our own hands, and must enforce the terms which our honor demands."

But it was not to be. Although the Northern people did not seriously oppose the purchase of sparsely populated States, such as California and New Mexico, they felt that the government of alien races was repugnant to republican institutions, colonization and Americanization being a condition precedent. Besides, there were other cogent objections. The annexation of Mexico meant prolonged military occupation, with a consequent increase of taxes, and the Northern people were already weary of a war to which they had given only a half-hearted support. The invasion of Mexico was a wanton and lustful act, and the successes of our arms never reconciled them to it. They had been fooled in respect to this thing from the beginning. The promised adjustment of the Oregon boundary — the slaveholders' sop to the North — was a trick. "54° 40' or fight" had had a craven ending.

But it was the impolitic efforts of the slave power to secure the fruits of their victory over Mexico that exhausted the patience of the North. By the treaty of Guadaloupe Hidalgo, Mexico ceded to the United States an area nearly equal to that of the thirteen original States. In this territory slavery had been abolished by Mexico, and, as the freesoilers contended, it could be restored only by act of positive law. Although the Northern people were not disposed to interfere with slavery in the accepted slave States, conceding it to be a vested customary right there, recognized by the organic law, and protected by the *lex loci*, they hated the system none the less, and determined that the new territories acquired from Mexico should never be polluted by traffic in human flesh. The slave power determined otherwise. What was the Mexican war for? If any doubt existed, the letter addressed by Mr. Trist to his chief, Secretary Buchanan, could officially dispel it. Mr. Trist had been sent to Mexico during the progress of the Mexican war, to negotiate a peace based upon the cession of New Mexico, the two Californias, and a right of way through the Isthmus of Tehuantepec, and he wrote as follows: —

"I concluded by assuring them (the Mexican Commissioners) that if it were in their power to offer me the whole territory described in our project, increased tenfold in value, and, in addition to that, covered a foot thick all over with pure gold, upon the single condition that slavery should be excluded therefrom, I could not entertain the offer for a moment, nor think even of communicating it to Washington."

Small wonder, then, that the Wilmot Proviso and kindred propositions should make the slaveholders gasp. All that bloodshed for nothing! Here was the beginning of the end. The slaveholders were filled with bitterness. A Democratic war had produced only Whig generals, one of whom, elected to the Presidency, had inflicted a parricidal stab by urging the admission of California as a free State. The gigantic stretch of country ceded by the treaty of Guadaloupe Hidalgo promised to be a barren acquisition. The Union stood upon the brink of dissolution. At last the chasm was bridged by a compromise. On the one hand, California was admitted as a free State, — an unavoidable concession, inasmuch as most of the gold hunters were from the North. On the other hand, the legislatures of the Territories of New Mexico and Utah were forbidden to enact any laws relating to slavery, and new States were to be admitted to the Union with or without slavery, as their respective constitutions should provide. After this the running was easy. The repeal of the Missouri Compromise logically followed; and all too quickly. The Northern people received this overt breach of faith as a threat against the perpetuity of free government which no sophistry could explain or condone. It was a sure presage of the awful storm. Thomas H. Benton, who, in current political matters was the best-informed man of his time, treats significantly of this crisis: —

"Up to Mr. Pierce's administration the plan had been defensive; that is to say, to make the secession of the South a means of self-defense against the abolition encroachments, aggressions, and crusades of the North. In the time of Mr. Pierce the plan became offensive; that is to say, to commence the expansion of slavery and the organization of territory to spread it over, so as to overpower the North with new slave States and drive them out of the Union. In this change of tactics originated the abrogation of the Missouri Compromise; the attempt to purchase one half of Mexico, and the actual purchase of a large part; the design to take Cuba; the encouragement to Kinney and Walker in Central America; the quarrels with Great Britain for outlandish coasts and islands; the designs upon the Tehuantepec, the Nicaragua, the Panama, and the Darien route; and the scheme to get a foothold in the island of San Domingo."

Herein we observe not so much a change of policy as an evolution thereof. Mr. Benton outlines with distinctness the future slave empire, towards which the South, in obedience to economic, social, and political conditions, had been tending for a half century. It is unnecessary to follow specifically his catalogue of events. It is sufficient to give a few details of the " grand movement " to which the slaveholders boastingly referred. Guadaloupe Hidalgo had not satisfied them; they must have more land! In a speech delivered in Congress upon the eve of the passage of the Kansas-Nebraska Bill, Mr. Benton threw light into dark places when he said : —

"What is a state secret in the city of Washington is street talk in the city of Montezuma. First. The mission of Mr. Gadsden to Santa Anna. It must have been conceived about the time that this bill was ; and, according to transpiring accounts, must have been a grand movement in itself, — $50,000,000 for as much Mexican territory on our Southern border as would make five or six States of the first class. The area of the acquisition, as I understand it, was to extend from sea to sea, on a line that would give us Santander, Monterey, Saltillo, Parras, Sonoro, and all lower California. This was certainly a large movement, both in point of money and of territory, and also large in political consequence; and clearly furnishing a theatre for the doctrine of non-intervention, if there should be any design to convert the newly-acquired territory from free soil, that it is, into slave soil, that it might be desired to be. Here, then, I believe I have found one branch of the grand movement; and although Mr. Gadsden returned from his mission with a small slice only of the desired territory, yet he has returned to his post, and may have better luck on a second trial, — if Santa Anna escapes from the speckled Indians (Los Indios Pintos) who have him at bay in the Sierra. I say nothing on the merits of this new acquisition, only that it is an old acquaintance with me, having first heard of it in November, 1846, and afterwards in March, 1848, at which latter time it was proposed in the Senate (by Mr. Davis, of Mississippi) on the ratification of Guadaloupe Hidalgo treaty; and rejected by the Senate. I voted against the Santander and Monterey line then; and have not seen cause to change my opinion. [Here Mr. Benton read the article proposed by Mr. Davis for the new line.] Secondly. The mission of Mr. Soulé to Madrid, — also a grand movement in itself, if reports be true, — two hundred and fifty millions for Cuba, and a rumpus is kicked up if the island is not got. . . . Mr. Chairman: I discuss nothing in relation to those rumored acquisitions of the island of Cuba and a broad side of Mexico; I only call attention to them as probable indexes to the grand movement of which the member from Georgia gave us the revelation, and which no one has denied."

Within eight years (1845-53) the slaveholders had added nearly 1,000,000 square miles of territory to the United States. When the disposition of the soil then acquired by them seemed likely to be unsatisfactory, they turned, naturally, to Cuba, where the status of slavery was beyond dispute. Buchanan endeavored, during a decade, to gain this island for the slave power. As Secretary of State under Polk, he offered one hundred millions of dollars for it, a proposition which met with short shrift. In 1854, as Minister to England, he signed the Ostend Manifesto, a collaboration which proclaimed to an astonished world the purpose of the United States to take Cuba *vi et armis*, if methods less arbitrary should not avail. In 1858, as President, he urged Congress to purchase the island, and Slidell introduced a bill appropriating thirty millions of dollars as a payment upon account; but this measure was never pressed to a vote. In 1860, both the Charleston and the Baltimore conventions indorsed the Cuban project.

Mr. Buchanan, in his zeal, was merely representative of the temper of the South. The convention which nominated him for President, in 1856, adopted as its own the doctrine of imperial conquest, by expressing sympathy with the efforts which were being "made by the people of Central America" to "regenerate the isthmus," and by resolving that it would expect that every proper exertion would be put forth to "insure our ascendency in the Gulf of Mexico."

In the light of this declaration, it is not strange that Stephen A. Douglas, as an aspirant for the Democratic nomination for the presidency, should deem it necessary to commit himself unreservedly to the policy of annexation. In New Orleans (1858) he said: "It is our destiny to have Cuba, and it is folly to debate the question. . . . Its acquisition is a matter of time only. . . . The same is true of Central America and Mexico. It will not do to say we have territory enough."

Meantime, those pioneers of Southern empire, the filibusters, were not idle. Lopez twice invaded Cuba, and died in an attempt to revolutionize it. The Order of the Lone Star, 28,000 strong, under the leadership of Governor Quitman, of Mississippi, had been enlisted for the same purpose. Expeditions such as these were the last convulsive efforts made by the slave power to extend its dominions. Walker invaded Central America, and reëstablished slavery in Nicaragua, but he could not maintain himself for long. It is said that he was aided in his conspiracy by Knights of the Golden Circle. Several years later (1860) this organization was intent upon the seizure of Guanajuato, the richest mining province of Mexico, if not of the world, when its plans were exposed by George D. Prentice, editor of the " Louisville Journal." The ritual of the society is typical, and it will be instructive to set out a part of it, including the obligation of the candidate for the first degree.

"Under the laws of 2 (Mexico) every emigrant receives from the state authorities a grant of 640 acres of land. Under a treaty closed with 3 (Manuel Doblado, Governor of Guanajuato), on the 11th of

February, 1860, we are invited to colonize in 2 (Mexico), to enable the best people there to establish a permanent government. We agree to introduce a force of 16,000 men, armed, equipped, and provided, and to take the field under the command of 3 (Doblado), who agrees to furnish an equal number of men to be officered by K. G. C.'s. To cover the original expenses of arming our forces, there is mortgaged to our Trustees the right to collect one half the annual revenues of 4 (Guanajuato), until we are paid the sum of $840,000. As a bonus there is also ceded to us 355,000 acres of land. The pay of the army is the same as the regular army of 2 (Mexico), which is about one eighth that of the United States. To secure this there is mortgaged to us all the public property of 4 (Guanajuato) amounting in taxable value to $23,000,000. 3 (Doblado) is now there making arrangements for our reception."

The initiate says that he will do all that he can, as an honorable man, to make "58 (a slave State) of 2 (Mexico)." As such he will "urge its 83 (annexation) to 72 (United States); otherwise he will oppose it with equal zeal." He will "sustain the effort to reduce the 88 (Peon system) to 89 (perpetual slavery)." "Until the whole civil, political, financial, and religious reconstruction of 2 (Mexico) has been completed, he will recognize 90 (limited monarchy) as the best form of 63 (government) for the purpose in view, since it can be made strong and effective." He further pledges himself to support no leader of the organization who will not swear " to extend 91 (slavery) over the whole 92 (Central America) if in his power. He shall try to acquire 93 (Cuba) and control 94 (the Gulf of Mexico)."

The Knights of the Golden Circle were to concentrate in "20 (Encinal County, Texas) by September 15, 1860 (a misprint, we presume, for 61. — Ed. of Journal), and will cross 5 (Rio Grande) by the first day of 6 (October)."

The " Louisville Journal " declared that nearly three thousand persons had been admitted into the order[1] in Louisville, a majority of them being non-residents.

---

[1] The Knights of the Golden Circle were variously styled, during a checkered career, The Circle, The Golden Circle, Circle of Honor, Knights of the Golden Circle, Knights of the Mighty Host, Order of American Knights, etc., etc. The late Senator Morton once said that this society changed its name as often as a thief, and pretty much for the same reasons. When the war began, it crossed the Ohio River, and

VII.

But filibustering expeditions were poor expedients, unless they should be supported by a vigorous and consistent policy of state; and this the slaveholders were unable to guarantee so long as they were subject to the restraints imposed by a union with a free North. Expansion — more land and more slaves — was the life of slavery; and its partisans must be in a position to map out and to carry out a comprehensive scheme of conquest. This was the purpose of secession, which could have no other sufficient object. The existing slave interests were not menaced, and needed no protection. Giddings tells us that, despite the vast amount of muddy assertion to the contrary, no bill, resolution, or other measure was introduced into either house of Congress, from the time of the formation of the Constitution to the civil war, which

found lodgment in Ohio, Indiana, and Illinois, where, after a brief and inglorious career, it died. It was succeeded by the Sons of Liberty, a formidable secret organization, whose object was the establishment of a Northwestern Confederacy.

looked to the abolition of slavery in any of the States where it existed. The Crittenden compromise beggared the South of all apology for seceding. It embodied the following propositions, to wit: Slavery to be recognized as existing in all the territory south of line 36° 30', to be perpetually free from interference by Congress, and to be protected as property during its continuance by all the departments of the territorial government. New States were to be admitted to the Union with or without slavery, as their constitutions should provide, — the pet doctrine of non-intervention. Congress was forbidden to abolish slavery in places under its exclusive jurisdiction and situated within slaveholding States. Officers of the government might bring their slaves to Washington city, and take them away. The transportation of slaves, whether by land, river, or sea, was to be unhindered. When a fugitive slave should be lost through the laches of an officer, or through the violence of a mob, the United States would pay the value of the slave to the owner. Although these propositions were in the form of five irrepealable amendments to the Constitution, they were contemptuously rejected by the irreconcilable Southern leaders. Secession was therefore not a defensive act; it was an aggression. Thaddeus Stevens (H. R., January 29, 1861) plumbed the purpose in these words: —

"The secession and rebellion of the South have been inculcated as a doctrine for twenty years past among slaveholding communities. At one time the tariff was deemed a sufficient cause; then the exclusion of slavery from free territories; then some violation of the fugitive slave law. Now, the culminating cause is the election of a President who does not believe in the benefits of slavery, or approve of that great missionary enterprise, the slave trade. The truth is, all these things are mere pretenses. The restless spirits of the South desire to have a slave empire, and they use these things as excuses. Some of them desire a more brilliant and stronger government than a Republic. Their domestic institutions and the social inequality of their free people naturally prepare them for a monarchy surrounded by a lordly nobility, for a throne founded on the neck of labor."

A war contrived for such a purpose could be the result only of a conspiracy, although this statement, as applied to the Rebellion, may seem to be incredible, when the magnitude of that struggle is considered. But it should not be forgotten that the slaveholders were working with plastic material. The Southern people were poor, as the result of a system which dishonored labor. They were confined and attached to locality, and they believed in states' rights. There was lack of social, mental, and commercial communication; of cities, of railroads, of newspapers, of schools, and of libraries. As Emerson said of slavery in the West Indies, "Slavery is no scholar, no improver. It does not love the whistle of the locomotive; it does not love the newspaper, the mailbag, a college, a book, or a preacher who has the absurd whim of saying what he thinks." The principal means of enlightenment were the political speeches delivered by the slaveholders, whose influence as the owners of land and labor was practically government; and the body of the Southern people, receiving their news and ideas at second-hand, came to reflect, with the faithfulness of a mirror, the hopes and the prejudices of their masters. The spirit of abolitionism, whenever it appeared, was exorcised by burning, hanging, shooting, or outlawing the person bewitched. As Mr. Cairnes has pointed out, the Southern people were the victims of the slave system. They were moulded to the invincible will of an intelligent, wealthy, unified, and desperate minority. From the beginning to the end of the war, they were the subjects of extraordinary delusions, being practiced upon with all the arts of chicanery known to ambitious and reckless politicians. Had they foreseen any one of the fatal consequences of their revolt against the government, — the four years of bloody strife, the depletion of their resources, the sacrifice of their personal rights, and the establishment of a military despotism shortly after the beginning of hostilities, — they could not have been tricked into secession by arbitrary and unrepresentative conventions, nor deluded into following the phantom of state sovereignty.

Promised relief from the "tyrannical usurpation" of the national government, they were cajoled into selling their modicum of liberty; assured of peaceful separation, they were defrauded into the most sanguinary conflict of modern times. They had been taught that the North was peopled by a vulgar race, greedy of gold, and destitute of honor and courage; while for the abolitionist was reserved a distinct place in their imaginations as the typical incarnation of all human villanies and vices. Him they hated; but all they despised.

Yes, they were assured, secession would be peaceable; revolution, holiday-making. And this confidence, which the leaders themselves partially shared, was seemingly justified by the aspect of affairs.

Before Mr. Lincoln was inaugurated on the 4th of March, 1861, secession was an accomplished fact in seven of the Southern States, and the government had not raised its hand. Nay, more, the President of the United States had sent a message to Congress, denying the power of the Federal government "to coerce a State into submission, which is attempting to withdraw or has actually withdrawn from the Union." War had been levied against the United States by the seizure of national forts, arsenals, sub-treasuries, custom houses, and other property; a United States vessel bearing reinforcements and provisions for Fort Sumter had been fired upon and driven out of Charleston harbor; in pursuance of an address issued by thirty Congressmen to their constituents from the capital of the nation, a provisional government had been organized at Montgomery, and a United States senator had resigned his seat to take the executive chair thereof. The treasury had been bankrupted; the navy had been scattered over distant waters; and arms and munitions of war in immense quantities had been removed to the South, where they had conveniently fallen into the hands of the belligerents. Even after the installation of the new administration, and in the face of these overt acts, the government kindly consented to notify South Carolina in case of any attempt to change the military status at Sumter.

Was the South so very wrong after all? The world looked on, and marveled. Through some alchemy of conscience, civil, military, and naval officers violated their trusts, and dishonored their allegiance. United States senators and representatives gravely argued a nation out of existence, lectured the passive North with solemnity on its shortcomings, in florid valedictories, expressive more of grief than of anger, drew their pay, and went South to dedicate "their lives, their fortunes, and their sacred honor" to the cause of human slavery. The situation recalls Carlyle's description of "a government tumbling and drifting on the whirlpools and mud deluges, floating atop in a conspicuous manner, no whither, like the carcass of a drowned ass." Apparently the greatest republic on earth, one which had been baptized in blood, had become impotent, and was about to die in a daze. Is it matter of surprise, then, that all Charleston should make high carnival of the bombardment of Sumter? Thus ended the ghastliest farce in the annals of history, and thus began the bloodiest of tragedies.

But the South, once committed to error, persevered in the face of defeat. Never, in an evil cause, did a great people fight more gallantly, nor endure more privations uncomplainingly. Spurred by the invincible spirit of their women, encouraged by the pious exhortations of their clergy, and goaded by the indomitable pride of their leaders, they fought the fight to the bitter end, recognizing only the remorseless fact of invasion, and neither reflecting on the past, nor speculating on the future. The star of empire was in its zenith. Success would have meant irretrievable ruin to the South. Already warfare had enthroned an absolute monarch, whom a pleasant fiction dominated a President. Victory would have deified him. Parliamentary government existed only in name. The Confederate Congress, whose meetings were mostly secret, sank into obscurity and neglect. The brain of the South was done with legislating, and had gone to fighting. The planters, who dominated before the war as land and slave owners, ruled with yet more masterful hand as military officers, and the people who had suffered the compulsion of drastic conscriptions, and who had been disciplined by army service, had become accustomed to yield unquestioning obedience to their ranking officers and to the central government. The theory of states' rights, used as a shield to cover a century's revolutionary designs, early fell into disrepute, and was revived later, in all simplicity, by North Carolina, only to disappear forever before the threat of martial law. Throughout the South, freedom of speech, freedom of the press, the right of trial by jury, all were gone. Independence achieved within the lines of original secession, the forms of Republican government might have been restored. But the soul was fled, and forever.

VIII.

It is impossible to trace in detail the great servile empire which once loomed so portentously, but which now belongs to shadow land. Certain things, may, however, be predicated. The new slave State would be essentially military in character. Born of a sleepless antagonism, it could never relinquish the sword. It would be isolated, contemned, and in a measure proscribed by the nations of the earth; but it would also be feared. Their enemies humbled in dust and blood, the slaveholders, arrogant' before, would become drunk with pride. Slavery vindicated by that might which makes right, they would proclaim her divinity to an infidel world, and would proselytize with a flaming scimitar. The Confederate legions, trained to victory by a great war, would be an irresistible army of conquest. The slave dominions would unfold like a fan, Maximilian's government would fall helplessly, even as it did fall, and the empire would coil itself unhindered about the Gulf of Mexico. Exhaustion of the soil, preservation against watchful enemies, and lust of power would steadily impel to territorial aggrandizement; and slavery, winding its way across the isthmus, would "find no limit but the Southern ocean." Nor is this all. The depletion of the labor force, counter colonization schemes by rival powers, and a proper fealty to the "divine institution" would compel also the revival of the foreign slave traffic, now truly a "missionary enterprise." Black slavers would spread their wings in flight, to hover, carrion-like, about the coasts of Africa, and communication between the two shores would for a time be rapid and constant. These conditions fulfilled, the dream would become reality, the slave nation empire. Truly, an empire! for a slave economy never differs from itself. A slave country cannot but be brutalized by its system of labor; the government of many, perhaps of the most, of its subjects is founded in force, not in consent; laws are imposed rather than agreed to; there is an intolerance of opinion and of peaceful arbitration of wrongs, and a violation of human rights which does not halt at the color line nor at political boundaries. Whatever its form, whatever its name, howsoever fair its beginnings, a slave government will degenerate into a despotism, orderly or capricious, as circumstances may determine. If it be a warring nation, — as the Southern empire must have been, owing to the predatory habits of its free population, the government of conquered peoples, and the hostility of free countries, — its head would be a dictator. There would be factious contentions with and among the nobles, and intervals of chaos, to be followed by the advent of a Cæsar, and by a remorseless absolutism.

And what of the North, left by secession a dishonored fragment? Would the free States bind about them more closely the ties of union, or would the principle of union be lost? Would the States upon the Pacific coast turn away from the pathless desert, and look beyond the ocean where their hope of commerce lay? Would the East separate from the West, and would the West join with the South? In the very heat of the war Vallandigham said: "There is not one drop of rain that falls on the whole vast expanse of the Northwest that does not find its home in the bosom of the Gulf. We must and we will follow it, with travel and trade; not by treaty, but by right; freely, peaceably; without restriction or tribute, under the same government and flag."

But the Mississippi could flow unvexed to the sea only under the black flag of slavery. Would commerce continue to follow the waterways, or would it be deflected east by artificial channels? Would there be custom houses at every border, and standing armies to enforce a right of way over adjacent territory? Would there be widespread commercial panics growing out of the enormous waste caused by the war of the Rebellion, and by unfavorable commercial and political conditions? Would new leagues or confederacies be formed which should possess the element of stability, or would they, too, be involved in strife and be torn with civil dissensions? It is not possible to measure the extent of the calamity. It might be more, or it might be less, but we know that it would be great. It is probable that freedom would still be a bond of union, that the States of the North, wearying of unworthy bickerings and petty jealousies, would gird themselves for a common purpose; that marriages made between free and slave States would be dissolved or would grow into a more perfect union by the elimination of slavery, and that the Northern idea would finally triumph, either in patient waiting, or in mighty conflict on blood-drenched fields.

The Southern empire would probably share the fate of Rome in its declining days. It would first lose the provinces outlying on the north either by military invasion, or, as surely, by the slow working of economic laws. The reopening of the slave trade would make slave-breeding unprofitable, and gradually the border States would fall away, subject, as they must be, to competition, and to other modifying influences of the Northern industrial system. Later, the other Southern States would be recovered to freedom, either through an increasing sterility of the land, or through a dearth of slave labor, caused by the ultimate suppression of the slave trade. Slavery would thus owe its destruction to one of two processes which secession might impede, but which it could not defeat. The slave empire would recede slowly towards the tropics, giving up all its old possessions in the republic, withering in the North, enlarging by tumorous growth in the South, until finally it should become an inert mass, be drained of its vitality, fade into a mere geographical expression, and perish of inherent weakness and decay. Or, perchance, the end would be hastened by foreign intervention. The slave empire, as a political idea and entity, would be a defiance of the moral sense of the civilized world, and would excite an international crusade, which, beginning on the coasts of Africa, might lay low the very citadel. In any event, the slave State would be doomed, whether it should die of itself or by the hand of the executioner. All this, however, after many, many years! And who can say what misery and disaster would be crowded into that hiatus of freedom! But it is useless to multiply hypotheses. Although we may not differ widely in our conclusions, our speculations are in air. We can only know that, a brief twenty-five years ago, the American Union, freighted with the best aspirations of humanity, narrowly escaped shipwreck, and that a great storm subsided into a billow of half a million of graves.

OXFORD.

OXFORD.

Oxford, "sweet city of dreaming spires," is England in miniature. It has been the seat of government, of learning, and of ecclesiastical agitation. Eight centuries are reflected in the glories of its architecture. Its halls and chapels are clustered memories.

On a clear night, when the gray of the buildings is silvered by the moonlight, and the shadows of the quaint lanes of Oxford are deepening, when "Great Tom" is

"Swinging slow with sullen roar,"

or, perchance, the bonny Christ Church bells are ringing out on the still air, a ramble through the "quads," deserted by all save their ghostly effigies, and in the gardens by the battered, ivy-mantled walls, melts the prose of life into poesy, and discovers to the imaginative the ecstasy of melancholy. The bells have ceased.

But in yonder chapel, whose windows are fretted with majestical fire, the swelling tones of the organ and the voices of the choristers rise in a flood of melody that reëchoes through the vaulted building, and with trembling cadence dies away in the silent night. Near are the cloisters, where the seed of learning was hidden long ago, and stealthily nourished to blossom out in after time into a goodly tree.

Oxford is one of the battle grounds of human thought, for peace hath its victories. It has been the cradle and grave of opinion. Great names stud its books, and clothe its history "with the beauty of a thousand stars." It has perspective and atmosphere. It is a vast storehouse of associations, and it speaks to the youth who throng its corridors, in various language. The impulses and aspirations, the intellectual prejudices and animosities, of each generation are here writ in stone, and the time-stained, yet time-defying walls still serenely stand to mock the defeated purposes of founders, and to average the vicissitudes of thought. Oxford has always been the mirror of the English mind, and all England has been the reflex of its agitations.

It was as fruitful a source of disturbance to the country in the past as is Moscow to Russia in the present. It has been the theatre of strife between the regular and secular clergy; between nominalism and realism; between scholasticism and the new learning; between Catholicism and Protestantism; between the civil and the common law. It was the headquarters of Charles I. during the revolution, and was long the seat of Jacobitism. Methodism and Tractarianism took their rise here. Although it has ceased to be the focus of political life, it is still the seed-plot of statesmen. In literature its influence was never so great as to-day.

The origin of the town, which is older than the university, may be dated back to the first centuries of the era. Situated on the Thames, Oxford was a defensive point against the inroading Danes, who pushed their way into the heart of England by the rivers, and was one of the most important of English boroughs. Then, as afterwards, it was the seat of the national councils, and a place of royal residence. It suffered severely in the Conquest, and shortly thereafter Oxford Castle was built by Robert D'Oigli, to whose tender mercies Oxfordshire had been committed by William the Conqueror. It was from this castle, on the night before its capitulation to King Stephen, that the Empress Maud fled over the snow and ice to Abingdon, clad in robes of white, and accompanied by three knights-of-arms.

Public teaching followed hard upon the Conquest, and was probably due to it, although before that time many scholars resided here. Learning naturally crystallized about the monasteries, and the Priory of St. Frideswide was perhaps the magnet which originally attracted the students. If this conjecture be wise, then the rise of the University of Oxford, like that of Salernum, the first of the universities of the Middle Ages, belongs to the great cenobite Order of St. Benedict. The admirable zeal of this order for the diffusion of secular learning has been attributed to the simplicity of its "knowingly unknowing and wisely unlearned" head, who, in enjoining his followers to collect books, forgot that all writings are not religious, and so, happily, proscribed none. After a while the Benedictine monks were displaced from St. Frideswide by the Augustinian canons, whose school became famous for its disputations or "Austins." And then came the Black and the Gray and the White Friars, with whom the university, when fully grown, waged war ceaselessly. The religious houses in Oxford belonging to the Abbeys of Abingdon and Eynsham should be mentioned in connection with the claustral schools of St. Frideswide as among the sources of the university. The story that Alfred founded this great seat of learning is imposing, but apocryphal. The name of the university is not mentioned in history before the Norman Conquest. The impulse to learning in Great Britain seems first to have come from Ireland, whose missionaries founded many monasteries. In the eighth and ninth centuries the most important place of teaching in England was the cathedral school at York, whither flocked the youth who had exhausted the capacity of lesser schools. To monastic institutions the world owes something. At the Abbey of Whitby, "the Westminster of Northumbrian kings," where the Roman and Irish churches had their fateful trial, Cædmon caught the inspiration of his song. The monastery of Jarrow was the hermitage of Bæda, the father of English history and learning. Dunstan was born near the monastery of Glastonbury, and afterwards became its abbot. Lanfranc and Anselm successively taught in the famous and fruitful Abbey of Bec. Macaulay compares the church with the ark, riding alone, " amidst darkness and tempest, on the deluge beneath which all the great works of ancient power and wisdom lay entombed, bearing within her that feeble germ from which a second and more glorious civilization was to spring." The services of the church are undoubted, and the figure is fine. But in justice it must be said that the church destroyed more manuscripts than she saved, and that the preservation of classical learning is due almost wholly to the cultivated tastes of the infidel Arab and Jew. When Latin became a dead language, all that was left of literature in the west was buried with it. It augured well, therefore, that the church, which dislikes innovation, should retain this language as a common vehicle of communication between the various countries of Europe.

But unfortunately the churchmen, who were the only learned men, were exclusively devotional. "Literature became religious, and, being religious, ceased to be literature." The church councils forbade the reading of pagan and secular books; taste declined; the classic models themselves were lost, owing to the scarcity of manuscripts, the indifference of custodians, and the absence of printing; and the love of learning became extinct. The Romano-Hellenic schools withered under imperial patronage and other influences, and western Europe fell into intellectual torpor, from which it was not fully aroused until the Protestant Reformation. There was a revival by Charlemagne, but it was short-lived. He established a palace school, and endeavored to raise the standard of teaching in the monasteries, those feeble survivals of the Romano-Hellenic schools. Half a century later, Alfred founded a palace school in England. But his work did not endure. He himself said that he knew of no priests south of the Thames who understood the meaning of the Latin prayers they used. In fact, the church was in a state of hopeless and sodden ignorance. Even the very bishops were illiterate. Such instruction as was given by the monasteries was sadly deficient in quantity and quality. These schools affected to teach the seven liberal arts of the Romano-Hellenic schools; the ancient trivium, consisting of grammar, rhetoric, and dialectics, and the quadrivium, consisting of music, arithmetic, geometry, and astronomy. According to the monkish distich, —

"Gramm. loquitur, Dia. vera docet, Rhet. verba colorat:
Mus. canit, Ar. numerat, Geo. ponderat, Ast. colit astra."

But in truth they did little of the sort. The arithmetic of Cassiodorus, the text-book commonly used, consisted of less than three folio pages. Grammar and rhetoric were scarcely more pretentious. Geometry was a crude outline. Music was reduced to church chants, and astronomy was limited to the calculation of Easter and festival days. Boys were taught to read and write, merely that they might study the Bible, and multiply copies of it. The object of education was purely religious, and temporalities were neglected. The world was to end in the year 1000. From the sixth century to the eleventh century, only two names, in the opinion of Hallam, are worthy of mention by the historian: Scotus Erigena, a student of Greek, who translated the pseudo-Dionysian writings, and who evolved a complete, though mystical system of philosophy; and Pope Silvester II., who was deeply educated in the Moorish schools, and who gained the papal chair — the voice of superstition whispered — through the intervention of the devil.

But with the twelfth century came the dawn. The rise of universities was only a part of a widespread movement, political and moral, which, to quote the compact statement of Laurie, showed itself "in the Order of Chivalry, in the Crusades, the rise of free towns, the incorporation of civic life, the organization of industries in the form of guilds, and, we may also add as another indication of the mental quickening, in the rise of a Provençal modern language and literature, and not a few heresies."

The cathedral and monastic schools, which were the only centres of learning in Europe, were the germs of the universities of the Middle Ages. These universities were a growth, and not a creation. They arose out of and grew up about the monasteries, which contained schools of two kinds : the inner or claustral school, reserved for the *oblati*, or those who intended to devote themselves to a monastic life, and the outer school, open to the *clerici* generally. At certain places, such as Oxford and Cambridge in England, and at Paris on the Continent, the attendance at these schools exceeded the limits of the monasteries, and there was an overflow of students into boarding halls or schools which were opened in the neighborhood by graduates, or by itinerant teachers. In Oxford, in the thirteenth century, there were more than seventy of these halls. Gradually the students freed themselves from monastic control, and formed learned communities of their own. They elected masters, prescribed their own government, and assumed sole jurisdiction of offenses committed by any of themselves. They became literary republics, independent of civic, civil, and papal power, the privileges which they assumed being formally recognized by letters patent or by papal decree. When their freedom was threatened by the covetousness of the municipality, the crown, or the Pope, they would jealously guard their own rights by playing off these powers against each other.

In the Middle Ages the term "universitas" implied no universality of study, nor indeed did it refer to it. The word meant "community," and was applied to any corporation, municipality, or guild. What we call a "university" was then known as a *universitas literaria* (learned community), which might contain subordinate *universitates* based upon nationality or upon a course of study. A *universitas literaria*, or a *studium generale*, as it was sometimes designated, was a privileged, self-governing school, which had specialized one or more studies, and which was open to all comers from any part of the world.[1] Thus, the arts' school at Salernum became a university when medicine was specialized by Constantinus, a great traveler who had translated many medical works from the Arabic. Students of various races and nations gathered here, where instruction was given in four languages, Greek, Arabic, Hebrew, and Latin, and where a *licentia medendi*, or license to practice the healing art, was conferred. Without the Saracenic influence which

---

[1] Vide Laurie's *Rise and Constitution of Universities*, Caput X.

led to the study of the liberal arts in Europe, the university movement would have been long deferred. The academies, universities, and libraries at Bagdad, Cairo, Cordova, Granada, and Seville were magnificent and famous, and were the resort of many students from the north, even from Oxford and Cambridge. Every library had its translators, and thus much of Greek literature was saved to us. At Bologna, Irnerius created a university by specializing the Roman law, and the beneficial influence of this revival it would be difficult to exaggerate. The new municipal and trade corporations, which had formed a cordon about feudalism, were seeking a definition of their property rights according to some coherent legal system, and while the Roman law was not considered favorable to political liberty, it was in other respects an admirable instrument of justice. Whatever its defects, its scientific precision was at least invaluable as a method. But in England it had a rival in the common law, which, though sometimes crude in its judgments and harsh in its penalties, was strong where the Roman law was weak. In 1149, Vacarius, of the university of Bologna, expounded the Roman law in Oxford, and this was the beginning of the strife between the two systems of jurisprudence. Vacarius was forbidden by King Stephen to continue his lectures, and afterwards the Parliament of Merton declared the immutability of the laws of England. But the civil law found an ally in the church. The political absolutism which tainted the Roman system was congenial to the priestly hierarchy, and the civil and canon laws soon became interwoven. The church objected to the common law because it was founded in the customs of the laity and not in the imperial constitutions. But the nobility and the people of England clung tenaciously to their own. Finally, in the reign of King Henry III., the church acknowledged defeat, by compelling the clergy to withdraw from the secular courts, where they alone were serving as the judges and the advocates. The civil law maintained its foothold in England only in the ecclesiastical courts, in the chancellors' courts of the universities, and in the High Court of Chancery. Students of the common law, thus excluded from Oxford and Cambridge, founded a seminary of their own at London, under the name of the Inns of Court and of Chancery, which flourished under the protection of the crown, and which to-day is the only portal of admission to the English bar.

Oxford must have attained much prominence as a seat of learning in the twelfth century to have attracted Vacarius from Italy. Universities had arisen over all western Europe, and, saving the University of Paris, Oxford was the most celebrated of them. Although there were few facilities of communication between these institutions which lay so widely apart, passionate devotees of learning, attracted by the fame of some great teacher, would find their way, on foot, from one place to another, many of them begging as they went. They gathered in thousands at the various universities, notably at Paris, at Bologna, at Oxford, and at Cambridge, where they divided into groups according to their political allegiance. The "nations" thus formed were a remarkable feature of university life in the Middle Ages, and were a fertile cause of strife. At Paris there were four nations, the Picard, the Norman, the French, — which included Italians, Spaniards, Greeks, and Orientals, — and the English, which embraced the English, Irish, Germans, Poles, and all others from the north of Europe. Each nation was independent, and exercised supervision of its own students and their lodging-houses. At Bologna the eighteen nations who represented countries north of the Alps coalesced into the *universitas citramontanorum*, and the seventeen southern nations formed the *universitas ultramontanorum*. Each nation elected a *consiliarius*, and the collective *consiliarii* of each *universitas* elected a rector. The government of the universities differed in detail, but the constitution of all of them was fundamentally democratic. The universities were distinct entities, claiming and obtaining sovereign rights. Bulls beneficial to them were frequently issued by the Popes, heresy being neither suspected nor dreaded. The privileges conferred by the crown upon the students included exemption from taxes, from military service, and from the jurisdiction of ordinary tribunals. The right to elect a rector was a custom shared by the trade guilds, and the immunity from civic authority was perhaps an extension of the right of benefit of clergy. Inasmuch as the universities of the Middle Ages owned no permanent buildings, and were possessed only of movable property, the students could keep the towns and the doctors in a state of subjection by threats of migration, and these threats were not idle.

Disputes at the University of Bologna led to the establishment of the University of Vicenza in 1204, and that of Padua in 1222. In Paris, owing to the youth of the students, many of whom attended the Notre Dame arts' school, out of which the university arose, the masters shared in the government. In Oxford there were two nations, the North and the South, and one procurator or proctor was chosen to represent each. Originally, the proctors were elected by the *regentes*, or teaching masters, who, in early times, constituted the sole legislature of the university. Afterwards, they were chosen by the whole body of the *regentes* and *non-regentes*. Chiefly, their duty was to keep the peace, and their authority extended even to the impeachment of the chancellor. Anciently, the chancellor was nominated by the Bishop of Lincoln, in whose see the town of Oxford lay; the church claiming jurisdiction of the university. Later, the convocation assumed the nominating power, subject, perhaps, to diocesan confirmation. To-day, the chancellor is but the nominal head of the university, and is a non-resident. His duties have devolved upon the vice-chancellor, who is elected biennially from a cycle composed of the heads of colleges. At Prague, a reorganization of the nations which gave the preponderance of power to the Slavs caused an emigration of the German teachers and pupils to Vienna, Erfurt, Heidelberg, and Leipsic. Thus began the German university system. In Paris, in 1221, a Town and Gown riot occurred, and, as Queen Blanche and the bishop favored the Town, certain students were expelled. The provost attacked the students at their games, and slew some who had not participated in the riot. Thereupon a large number of masters and pupils left Paris for Orleans, Toulouse, and Oxford. It was only after this secession that Oxford ceased to be an arts' school, and became a university. It, too, suffered from three secessions within a century, — to Reading, to

Northampton, and to Stamford, — but it survived them all. The cause of the secession to Northampton has been referred to the rebellion of the sturdy Earl Simon, who held his parliament in Oxford, and with whom the northern students sided. But an excuse for strife was never lacking. The times were troublous, and full of sleepless feuds. Gown was noisy, lawless, and supercilious, and Town smote Gown whenever chance offered. On St. Scholastica's day, February 10, 1354(5), there was a bloody fray, in which the Town was reinforced by the Country. "Slea, slea! havock, havock! smyt fast! give gode knocks!" was the battle-cry. Fourteen halls were plundered, forty scholars were killed, and the university was left deserted. For this grievous deed the town was laid under interdict by the bishop, and was shorn of many of its privileges by the crown. The assize of bread and wine and the supervision of weights and measures were taken from it, and were invested in the university. Nor did the humiliation end here. For nearly five centuries thereafter, by a decree of the king, the mayor, the bailiffs, and sixty leading citizens were obliged to attend mass in St. Mary's, the university church, on each anniversary of St. Scholastica's day, and there to offer at the high altar one penny each (a goodly sum then), of which two thirds were to be distributed at once among the poor scholars.

In the Middle Ages, Oxford was a walled town, extending one half mile one way and one fourth of a mile another, and within this area it is said that twenty thousand students were crowded. This number is largely overstated, although it is probable that the attendance in the time of Roger Bacon was much greater than it is now. The monasteries and cathedral schools were being deserted for the universities, even cooks and servitors were enrolled, and many young scholars attended the grammar schools at Oxford, as the licenses for "fetchers" and "bringers" indicate. Chaucer, in his delicious verse, gives us a contemporary portrait of the Oxford student of those days: —

> "A clerk ther was of Oxenford also,
> That unto logik hadde longe i-go.
> As lene was his hors as is a rake,
> And he was not right fat, I undertake;

> But lokede holwe, and therto soberly.
> Ful thredbar was his overest courtepy.
> For he hadde geten him yit no benefice,
> Ne was so worldly for to have office.
> For him was levere have at his beddes heede
> Twenty bookes, clad in blak or reede,
> Of Aristotle and his philosophye,
> Then robes riche, or fithele, or gay sawtrye.
> But al be that he was a philosophre,
> Yet hadde he but litel gold in cofre;
> But al that he mighte of his freddes hente,
> On bookes and on lernyng he it spente,
> And busily gan for the soules preye
> Of hem that yaf him wherwith to scoleye;
> Of studie took he most cure and most heede.
> Not oo word spak he more than was neede,
> And that was seid in forme and reverence
> And schort and quyk, and ful of high sentence.
> Sownynge in moral vertu was his speche,
> And gladly wolde he lerne, and gladly teche."

Within the walls was a seething mass of tempestuous life. There were thousands of boys huddled in bare lodging-houses, "clustering around teachers as poor as themselves in church-porch and house-porch, drinking, quarreling, dicing, begging at the corners of the streets. . . . Scholars from Kent and scholars from Scotland wage the bitter struggle of South and North.

At nightfall roysterer and reveler roam with torches through the narrow lanes, defying bailiffs, and cutting down burghers at their doors. Now a mob of clerks plunges into the Jewry, and wipes off the memory of bills and bonds by sacking a Hebrew house or two. Now a tavern row between scholar and townsman widens into a general broil, and the academical bell of St. Mary's vies with the town bell of St. Martin's in clanging to arms. Every phase of ecclesiastical controversy and political strife is preluded by some fierce outbreak in this turbulent surging mob. When England growls at the exactions of the Papacy, the students besiege a legate in the abbot's house at Osney. A murderous Town and Gown row precedes the opening of the Barons' War. 'When Oxford draws knife,' runs the old rhyme, ' England's soon at strife.' "[1]

With the advent of the collegiate system the brawls became less frequent. Decency and order were enforced, and the unattached students or "chamberdeykins," the leaders in lawlessness, were suppressed by statute. But this was not all of the reform. The colleges superseded the

[1] Green's *Short History of the English People*, pp. 158, 159.

religious houses, which, in the early days of the university, were the most spacious and comfortable buildings in Oxford. Gradually, too, the number of licensed halls diminished, until now but few remain. Then, as now, the university was a distinct corporation, which included the colleges and halls but was not included by them, and it is possible to-day (by recent enactment), as it was in the days of the chamberdeykins, to be an unattached member of the university.

Merton College, founded by Walter de Merton, in 1264, was the first college structure erected in Oxford, and was the model of the English college system. The statutes drawn by the founder were characterized by such wisdom and foresight that they remained practically unaltered during seven centuries. Merton's object was anti-monastic, the cultivation of lay learning, and the upbuilding of a secular class. Although the discipline prescribed was severe, and ascetic in character, the students were forbidden ever to take vows, and were required to study philosophy and the liberal arts before beginning theology. Merton, in projecting his college, is said to have had in mind the Sorbonne, a college of the University of Paris, founded by the chaplain of Louis IX. fourteen years before. In Oxford, two colleges besides Merton were established in the thirteenth century, University and Balliol, and thereafter colleges appeared at irregular intervals, averaging about one to every generation.

Balliol College owes its foundation to a woman. About 1260, John Balliol, son of the King of Scotland of that name, made certain payments for the support of poor students at Oxford, but it remained for his widow, Lady De Vorguilla, to execute the trust by organizing, in 1282, "The House of the Scholars of Balliol." In her charter deed Lady De Vorguilla conceded the principle of self-government, and refused to place legal restrictions upon elections to the foundation. Although established by a Scot, the college was not restricted to the Scotch, and, contrary to the custom of the times, it was not made the mere appanage of any district, abbey, or institution. It was open to the world. De Vorguilla's object, like that of Walter De Merton, was to found a home for secular learning, and, in the case of Balliol, divinity was not even taught in the institution until the fourteenth century. The foundation may, therefore, be regarded as a protest against the exclusive ecclesiasticism of the times.

The most notable creation of the fourteenth century was New College, the benefaction of William of Wykeham, Bishop of Winchester. He had been the architect of Windsor Castle, and he did not fail to impress his art upon the walls of his Oxford foundation. New College obtained its name because it was a revelation to the college world of comfort, convenience, and architectural beauty. The spacious cloisters, the lofty tower, and the noble chapel are enshrined in gardens of exquisite beauty, whose "sweet, sacred, stately seclusion" afford a refuge to the musing scholar and the dreaming poet.

The colleges justified the expectations of their creators in developing nearly all of the men who gave distinction to the university. When scholasticism reached its second stage, in the translation of the works of Aristotle into Latin, Oxford gained fame for subtle disputation, and became preëminent among the educational institutions of the Western world. Anthony Wood, an historian of Oxford, who flourished four centuries ago, asks, with the pride of an ardent lover, "What university, I pray, can produce an invincible Hales, an admirable Bacon, an excellent, well-grounded Middleton, a subtle Scotus, an approved Burley, a resolute Baconthorpe, a singular Ockham, a solid and industrious Holcot, and a profound Bradwardin? all of which persons flourished within the compass of one century. I doubt that neither Paris, Bologna, nor Rome, that grand mistress of the Christian world, nor any place else, can do what the renowned Bellosite (Oxford) hath done."

Now was the golden age of the universities, the heralds of the coming day. Knowing no race, nor creed, nor country, they formed a cosmopolitan league of learning that threatened the isolation of feudalism. Rich and poor, noble and peasant, Christian and infidel, Aryan and Semite, stood upon a level. There was but one aristocracy, that of the intellect. Truly a grand epoch, and a fine ideal for so long ago, that promised great things for the future. But, alas! the votaries of learning were to go through an ordeal of fire, sweat, blood, and agony before they should come into undisputed possession of their realm.

The first scholar to earn the rebuke of the church, was Scotus Erigena, who revived the Platonic theory of Universals (with an infusion of Aristotelianism). He was accused of pantheism, which was the legitimate outcome of his realism. Two centuries later, the discussion was begun anew by Roscelin and Anselm, nominalist and realist respectively, and thereafter it raged violently in the schools for three hundred years. Roscelin's advocacy of nominalism or individualism led him to deny the doctrine of the Trinity, and for this he was summoned before the Council of Soissóns, where he was forced to recant. His pupil, Abelard, who took a *via media* between realism and nominalism, signally discomfited William of Champeaux, at Paris, and ruled in his stead at the university. His lectures attracted thousands of students, including many from Oxford. In combating the anti-Trinitarian views of Roscelin, he himself fell under the ban of the church council; nor was this the sum of his offending. His book, "Sic et Non," a compilation of the antinomies of the Fathers, was regarded as an heretical attempt to apply logic to theology. When Abelard forsook Paris for a desert place in Champagne, he took the most of the university with him; nor, indeed, could he rest there. But everywhere multitudes heard him, for in those days students were eager. Abelard knew little of the works of Aristotle, which were transmitted to Europe at last through the helping hands of Nestorians, Arabs, and Jews. Hales, the Doctor Invincible of Oxford, was the first schoolman acquainted with all of them, and Grostête, also of Oxford, was among the first to expound them from the original Greek. Aristotle was accepted by a protesting church as a logician, and afterwards, even more reluctantly, as a metaphysician. In 1209, a synod held in Paris ordered his metaphysical volumes to be burned.

In vain, however. Thomas Aquinas, the Angelic Doctor, and the mendicant orders succeeded in Aristotelianizing the church. The Thomists, who included the Dominicans and Augustinians, and the Scotists or Franciscans, warred bitterly with each other over metaphysical niceties, even as did the Jansenists and Jesuits of later days. The Scotists favored free will, the Thomists a moderate determinism; the *quidditas* or "whatness" and the *hacccitas* or "thisness" of the individual, which became involved in the problem of universals, were also the subjects of heated controversy. Duns Scotus, who was a pupil of Merton College, Oxford, and a Franciscan, won the title of *Subtilis*, it is said, by refuting nearly two hundred objections which were urged by the Thomists against the doctrine of the Immaculate Conception. Under his influence the University of Paris formally disapproved the position taken by his opponents.

Next, out of Oxford, came William of Ockham, the pupil and rival of Duns Scotus, and the greatest of the scholastics. To him belongs the honor practically of ending the discussion of the question of universals, now nearly seventeen hundred years old, and seemingly everlasting. He maintained that universals (general ideas or abstractions) had no objective existence (*ante rem* or *extra animam*), but were only *in mente*. "Ockham's razor"—"*Entia non sunt multiplicanda præter necessitatem*"—was a protest against the purely deductive mental processes of the scholastics. You cannot derive the individual from the universal. You must begin with the singular and rise to the general. His writings breathed the spirit of induction, the acceptance of which was the beginning of the modern world. Ockham opposed that perfect representative of scholasticism, Thomas Aquinas, by proclaiming the divorce of theology and philosophy. In several things he anticipated Wycliffe. He attacked the temporal sovereignty of the Pope, and pleaded for the independence of the crown. He inveighed against the luxury of the Franciscans, combating the opinions of Pope John XXII. (he whose simony Dante condemned through the mouth of St. Peter in the Paradiso) at a time when the University of Paris was cringing to obtain his patronage. Ockham was tried for heresy, and was imprisoned by the Pope at Avignon for seventeen weeks, whence he escaped to Munich. In 1339, his works were condemned by the University of Paris, but time vindicated him in the acceptance of the doctrine of nominalism as an orthodox tenet.

Ockham had sounded the death knell of scholasticism. That system failed because it had ignored induction and had endeavored to arrive at truth by internal light alone. It rendered a service in teaching the human mind to reason acutely from given premises, but the value of this service must be estimated moderately. The world has not gone wrong so much because of illogical reasoning as because the data upon which that reasoning was based have been false or insufficient, and therefore misleading. The scholastics chose premises to which it was not possible to apply the test of reason. All things seem to have been equally probable in an age whose mental characteristics were astrology, magic, alchemy, Neoplatonism, the patristic writings, and Aristotelianism. The schoolmen "tied and untied the same knot, and formed and dissipated the same cloud," debating propositions for whose terms there were no corresponding ideas. In the latter days of scholasticism some frivolous and silly questions were asked and discussed: Can one angel occupy two places, or can two angels occupy one place at the same time? Was the head formed for the brain or for the eye? Has a rat, which has eaten of the Host, thereby partaken of Christ's body? Fanciful coincidences, such as that of the two horns of the beetle and of the moon, were treated as relations. The inherent weakness of the schoolmen was their ignorance of the laws of evidence, which, preferring a natural to a strained or mystical explanation of phenomona, were first practically applied in Europe by the medical and legal professions.

Scholastic philosophy lingered long because it satisfied the taste for contention, and it served at least two ends: it sharpened the tools of thought by endowing the vulgar languages with "precision and analytic subtlety," and it inaugurated the age of discussion. It found an arena in the universities where teaching and disputation were public and oral. Knowledge was meagre, although there was much love of it, and progress was small because the refinements of theology absorbed the attention of the subtlest minds. The only intellectual career lay in or through the church, and theology offered the highest rewards. Those who devoted themselves to it used as text-books the "Sentences" of Peter the Lombard, and the "Summa" of Aquinas. Those who followed the law studied Justinian and Gratian; while in medicine, Galen and Hippocrates were the chief authorities.

In mathematics, Roger Bacon complained that few pupils crossed the *pons asinorum* of Euclid, and this was true for long afterwards. He said also that he could communicate in a half year to any intelligent person what it had cost him forty years to acquire; and this was, perhaps, less a reflection upon the methods of teaching in vogue, than upon the pitiful lack of knowledge. Education was gained under immense disadvantages in those days. There was no university press which could print and bind the whole Bible in twelve hours. There was not even a translation of the Bible. Manuscripts were brought from afar, and were precious in their rarity. One cannot listen without a pang to Bacon's wail for mathematical instruments, astronomical tables, and books.

The scarcity of manuscripts has been considered an effect of ignorance as well as a cause, and it has been intimated that the monks were not so actively employed in copying as has been supposed. After the conquest of Egypt by the Saracens, the exportation of papyri ceased.

Writing material became very costly, and valuable books were lost to posterity through erasures for new writings. Many monasteries possessed only one missal. The Countess of Anjou paid for a copy of the Homilies of Haimon, Bishop of Halberstadt, two hundred sheep, five quarters of wheat, and the same of rye and millet. To a later and unregenerate generation the price seems high. Louis XI. could not borrow a work of Rasis, the Arabian physician, from the Faculty of Medicine of Paris without pledging a good deal of plate, and without getting a nobleman to go his surety for a large amount. From this it may be inferred either that books were rare and dear, or that the faculty knew the king. From the Jews of Oxford, Roger Bacon obtained manuscripts which helped him in his scientific researches. The life of this man, the pioneer of experimental science and exponent of induction, was long and troubled. Greeted as Doctor Mirabilis in Paris, he returned to Oxford and joined the Franciscans. Here he was accused of practicing the black arts, and was interdicted from lecturing by the general of his order. A ban was placed upon his writings, and he was sent back to Paris, where he remained under strict religious surveillance for ten years. At last, Guy de Folques, a churchman of culture, ascended the papal chair. He ordered Bacon to write a treatise for him upon the sciences. This was the long-sought opportunity, and Bacon was eager to grasp it. But he had spent his whole fortune and that of his family, in his scientific investigations, and was impoverished. Finally, his friends came to his rescue by pawning their goods, and he set to work with such vigor that in eighteen months he completed, under extraordinary difficulties, the Opera Majus, Minus, and Tertium. These he forwarded to the Pope by a trusty messenger, but it is not certain that he received a reply. Some years after, in consequence of having written a protest against clerical vices and ignorance, he was thrown into prison, where he was confined for fourteen years. Shortly after his release he died, with these pathetic words upon his lips: "I repent now that I have given myself so much trouble for the love of science."

When Bacon was at Oxford, he used as a laboratory and observatory a pharos of Stephen, erected on Folly Bridge. This tower was removed in 1779, an act of vandalism which evoked the following verses : —

> "Roger, if, with thy magic glasses
> Kenning, thou seest below what passes,
> As when on earth thou didst descry
> With them the wonders of the sky;
> Look down on your devoted walls,
> Oh, save them, ere thy study falls,
> Or to thy votaries quick impart
> The secret of thy magic art ;
> Teach us, ere learning 's quite forsaken,
> To honor thee and — save our Bacon."

The past has an irresistible charm. Its defects are hidden by a poetic haze. It is certain, however, that mediæval Oxford could not have been very inviting. The streets were unpaved and almost unlighted. The ways were narrow and the traffic dangerous. Candles were too costly to use, and men could not read by rushlights. In consequence, the day began and ended with the coming and going of the sun. "There was an absence of all due means of cleanliness and health. . . . The dining halls were strewn with rushes, into which all sorts of nastiness were thrown. After about a fortnight they became unendurable; and there was, or ought to have been, a general cleaning. The sweating sickness of Tudor times, like other plagues, was largely due to the filthy mode of living." [1]

It is not surprising that Oxford was scourged frequently with pestilence, and that plays were forbidden as attracting crowds who spread infection. When Edward III. was a prince and a pupil in Balliol College, Oxford, he was attacked by the small-pox. Doctor Gaddesden of Merton College, who attended him, recommends the following treatment: "Cause the whole of the body of your patient to be wrapped in red scarlet cloth, or any other red cloth. Command everything about the bed to be made red. This is an excellent cure." Red, as resembling the color of the blood, was invested with high curative powers, according to a doctrine of analogies which prescribed eye-bright for diseases of the eye. Bodily ills were supposed often to be the result of dæmonic visitation, and to call for ecclesiastical remedies. Hence the favor ac-

---

[1] Historic Town Series : Boase's *Oxford*, p. 60.

corded to shrine, miracle, and relic cures. St. Valentine cured epilepsy; St. Gervasius, rheumatism; St. Judas, coughs; St. Ovidius, deafness; St. Hubert, hydrophobia. One method of expelling the dæmons was to make the human body uninhabitable by the taking of loathsome mixtures, such as garlic, fennel, livers of toads, blood of rats, fibres of the hangman's rope, etc. But generally material remedies were disapproved by the church. Three councils in the twelfth century warned churchmen against having anything to do with the profession of medicine, and in the thirteenth century Pope Innocent III. commanded physicians to call in ecclesiastical advice in all cases. The University of Salernum was regarded with suspicion, although even there saintly relics as well as medicine were relied upon to heal the sick. It was the age of magic. The doctrine of resurrection forbade dissection, and surgery was impious as involving bodily dismemberment. In Oxford, so late as the time of James II., many people were touched for the king's evil; but it is pleasant to record that, long before, the hard-headed Queen Elizabeth was skeptical as to the efficacy of her powers, despite fervid assurances given to her by her chaplain. Charles II., it is said, touched nearly one hundred thousand persons.

In the fourteenth century there appeared in Oxford a man who was to take up the work of Ockham and Bacon, and to earn for himself the proud distinction of the first Protestant, — John Wycliffe. He attacked the citadel of ecclesiasticism itself. He proclaimed the innocence of honest error; he denied the headship of the Roman Church, the supremacy of St. Peter as compared with the other apostles, and the temporal sovereignty of the Pope. He disliked the friars, because, he said, they were the emissaries of a power across the seas; and he mocked their gluttony by establishing a fraternity of poor priests, who went everywhere to preach and to pray among the lowly. It would probably have gone hardly with Wycliffe, had not the church at this time made a demand for the papal tribute, which had been in arrears for thirty-three years. This demand the king and Parliament refused to meet, and Wycliffe was asked to publicly defend the position taken. He maintained the supremacy of the king and Parliament over ecclesiastics as well as civilians, — a revolutionary doctrine which gained wide support by reason of a well-founded belief that the papacy at Avignon was aiding the French king in his wars against England with money supplied by the English people. Wycliffe thus became the embodiment of nationalism.

Afterwards, he denounced transubstantiation, thereby strengthening his argument, as it was the administration of the sacrament that elevated the poorest priest above the crowned head. The church repeatedly demanded that the University of Oxford should condemn Wycliffe's tenets, and even to surrender his body; but this demand was steadily refused. The great university made noble answer through its head, Chancellor Rugge: "No bishop or archbishop has any authority whatever over the university in matters of belief." Oxford became a "nest of heretics." Ultimately, Wycliffe lost power with the state, when his movement assumed a political character. Wat Tyler's uprising was attributed to him; and the university, on pain of forfeiture of all liberties and privileges, yielded to a command to displace its obnoxious chancellor and proctors. This concession served as an evil precedent. Even Lincoln College was founded by the bishop of the diocese, as "a little college of theologians to help in ruining heresy." In the course of time Jesus College was instituted by Hugh Price, to counteract the influence of Lincoln, for thus did opinion play at see-saw in Oxford.[1] Renewed commissions failed to extirpate heresy in the university, which was covert and stubborn. The mendicant order established by Wycliffe grew formidable, was persecuted, and was almost extinguished, although, after the passing of a century, we hear Erasmus ironically expressing the hope that either "Lollardism or persecution would stop before winter, for it raised the price

[1] Concerning the founder of Jesus College there is this epigram:—

>"Hugo Preesh
>Built this Collesh
>For Jesus Creesh
>And the Welsh Geesh
>Who love a peesch
>Of toasted cheesh
>And here it ish."

Moore's *Historical Handbook*, p. 48. A book full of curious matter.

of fire-wood." Despite papal bulls and anathemas, Wycliffe died in his bed; but after his bones had rested thirty years in their grave, they were exhumed by order of the Council of Constance, and burnt. They were burnt too late! The ashes were "cast into the brook, whence," his followers said, "they reached the sea, and thus the whole world became his sepulchre." And it was so. His writings were carried by wandering students over all Europe, and led to the Hussite revolt in Bohemia, the prelude to the Reformation. The crowning achievement of Wycliffe's life was his translation of the Vulgate into language which the people spoke and understood. Abandoning the scholastic Latin, he became the father of English prose, even as Chaucer, his contemporary, became the father of English poetry. Until Wycliffe's time French was the language of fashion and of the law; and we find a statute of Oriel College, Oxford, as late as 1325, enjoining the students to speak in Latin or in French. Nevertheless, Oxford had much to do with forming English prose. Wycliffe's successor, William Tyndale, who published a translation of the

New Testament and of the Pentateuch in 1526, studied in Magdalen Hall (afterwards Hertford College). His translation, and that of Wycliffe, "the common ancestor" of all English editions, were largely the basis of the King James version, the making of which was suggested by an Oxonian. To the committee who translated the King James version, Oxford contributed fourteen members, and in the revision made recently the university was also represented.

But the path of the new learning was rugged, and was weirdly lighted by the flames of living funeral pyres. William Tyndale was tried for heresy, and strangled, his body being given to the fire. And other punishments less merciful were employed. Campanella was imprisoned twenty-seven years, and seven times put to the torture. "Free thought was a crime," but not for always. It is the pride of Oxford to have nurtured some of those brave spirits who furthered that great intellectual renaissance, the Protestant Reformation, a movement which wrought among other things the reform of the Catholic Church itself. Grocyn, Linacre, and Colet, Oxford students, had drunk thirstily at the fountains of the new learning in Italy during the era of Lorenzo the Magnificent, and upon their return to Oxford they revived the study of the Greek language and literature, and sounded the note of religious reformation. Colet, ignoring the schoolmen, invested the Scriptures with a new meaning, giving to them a plain, common-sense interpretation. Deeply impressed with the iniquities which he saw at Rome, he denounced the Pope as "wickedly distilling poison to the destruction of the church," and demanded a purification of the whole clerical system. He gained two notable disciples and associates, Thomas More and Erasmus. This remarkable group may be described in Erasmus' own words: "When I listen to my friend Colet, it seems to me like listening to Plato himself. In Grocyn, who does not admire the wide range of his knowledge? What could be more searching, deep, and refined than the judgment of Linacre? Whenever did nature mould a character more gentle, endearing, and happy than Thomas More's?" Erasmus went from Oxford to Italy to study Greek, and thus to prepare himself for his great work. When he came back to England, he published his "Praise of Folly," a stinging satire on the clergy, which he wrote in More's house in London; and his translation of the Greek Testament, done in Cambridge, in which the Latin and Greek texts were arranged in parallel columns. These works created a great sensation throughout Europe, the latter having far-reaching consequences. The translation was read by Luther, and elicited a tribute of admiration from Melancthon. It undermined the belief in the absolute inspiration of the Vulgate version of the Bible, and thereby shook the authority of the church. Colet went to London, where he was made Dean of St. Paul's, and where he taught the new learning in a school which he founded. Sir Thomas More preached democracy and religious toleration in his "Utopia." When the papal bull denouncing Luther reached Germany, and the Elector of Saxony was ordered to surrender the heretic, the elector took counsel of Erasmus, asking him what he really thought of Luther. Erasmus laconically summed up the situation thus: "Luther," he said, "has committed two crimes. He has hit the Pope on the crown and the monks on the belly." The elector did not deliver up Luther, and Luther burned the bull. The Oxford and the Wittenberg reformers were helpmeets, their point of agreement being the need of the immediate reformation of the church. But in other respects their differences were radical. Oxford, as Mr. Seebohm points out in his charming book, was far in advance of Wittenberg. Luther was a lineal descendant of the schoolmen, Wycliffe and Huss, and, in accepting their Augustinianism, he adhered to the scholastic or dogmatic system of theology. The basis of this theology was, first, "the plenary inspiration of each text contained in the Scriptures; and, secondly, the existence of an ecclesiastical authority of some kind capable of establishing theological hypotheses; so that, in this respect, Luther and other Augustinian reformers, instead of advancing beyond the Oxford reformers, have lagged far behind." The result was, that " the Protestant movement, whilst accomplishing by one revolutionary blow many objects which the Oxford reformers were striving, and striving in vain, to compass by constitutional means, has been so far antagonistic to their work in other directions as to throw it back, — not to say to wipe it out of remembrance, — so that in this nineteenth century those Christians who have desired, as they did, to rest their faith upon honest facts and not upon dogmas, upon evidence and not upon authority, instead of taking up the work where the Oxford reformers left it, have had to begin it again at the beginning, as Colet did at Oxford in 1496. They have had, like the Oxford reformers, to combat at the outset the theory of 'plenary inspiration,' and the tendency inherited along with it from St. Augustine, by both schoolmen and Protestant reformers, to build up a theology, as I have said, upon unverified hypotheses, and to narrow the boundaries of Christian fellowship by the imposition of dogmatic creeds so manufactured."[1] The diffusion of secular learning went on apace, and the gulf between the old and the new widened. Hebrew and Greek were denounced by churchmen as heretical tongues, and in Oxford two parties were formed, the Greeks and the Trojans. The enmity of the conservatives was bitter, as Vives testifies. He was invited from

---

[1] Seebohm's *Oxford Reformers*, pp. 494, 496, 497.

Spain to teach Greek in Corpus Christi, a college which was the first fruit of the classical revival. He says, "I must take care of my health, especially here, where, if I were to fall ill, I should be cast out upon a dung-hill, and where there would be no one who would regard me better than a vile, diseased dog."

Later in the century another and greater critic of Aristotelianism, Giordano Bruno, came to Oxford to take part in a dialectical tournament, which was one of the features of a fête given by the Earl of Leicester, Chancellor of the University, to the County Palatine, Albert de Lasco; for such was the manner of the time. Bruno claims that he stopped the mouth of his adversary fifteen times; it is certain that he gave great offense by his arrogance. Afterwards, while delivering a course of lectures, he was indiscreet enough to deride the authorities, and to style them "a constellation of pedants," which put an end to his connection with the university. Aristotelianism was statutory at Oxford, as it was in the University of Paris and in the church. The universe was a closed sphere, with an immobile earth as its centre.

Bruno declared that there was an infinity of worlds. He asserted also the diurnal revolution of the earth. Copernicus, Bruno, Galileo, Kepler, and Newton are the order of a noble progression, and the issue presented by them was momentous. The establishment of the heliocentric doctrine was a cataclysm of thought. It dethroned man as the sovereign of created things. The stars in their beauty were not made to give him light. His world was but a point in the infinite; it was a satellite, and not a sun. All this involved a denial of the infallibility of the church, the overshadowing power of Christendom, and the assertion of the supremacy of human reason. Galileo was compelled to bend his knees before the cardinals, and to curse and to abjure the heliocentric doctrine; Bruno's free spirit went up in flame. But persecution was not wholly Catholic. Oxford suffered sadly during the whole period of religious reformation. A visitation instituted by Henry VIII., a too zealous convert to the new learning, suppressed the study of the canon law, and scattered the leaves of the scholastic writings about the quadrangles. "Dunce" (Duns Scotus) was "set in Bocardo" (as the saying went), a prison which surmounted the north gate of the town. Mr. Boase ingeniously suggests that the singular name of this place of confinement may have been adapted sarcastically from the "syllogism called Bocardo, out of which the reasoner could not 'bring himself back into his first figure' without the use of special processes." In the reign of Edward VI. religious reformation almost emptied the university. There were two visitations, and "not only were the old services abolished, but altars, images, statues, 'the things called organs,' and everything else which seemed to savour of 'superstition,' were defaced or swept away. . . . 'Cartloads' of classical and scientific manuscripts were consigned to the flames, together with many an illuminated masterpiece of scholastic literature."[1]

Under Mary there was burning of bodies as well as of books. Opposite Balliol College, of which at one time Wycliffe was the head, stands a memorial to the Protestant martyrs, Cranmer, Archbishop of Canterbury, and Bishops Latimer

---

[1] G. C. Brodrick, Warden of Merton, *A History of the University of Oxford*, p. 81.

and Ridley, who were burned in Bloody Mary's reign near this spot. Latimer and Ridley stood side by side in death, and, as the flames mounted, Latimer spake in these words: "Be of good comfort, Master Ridley, and play the man. We shall this day light such a candle by God's grace in England as I trust shall never be put out." Cranmer witnessed the execution from Bocardo, and perished six months later at the same stake. "Fire being now put to him, he stretched out his right hand and thrust it into the flame, and held it there a good space, before the fire came to any other part of his body; where his hand was seen of every man sensibly burning, crying with a loud voice, 'This hand hath offended.' As soon as the fire got up, he was very soon dead, never stirring nor crying all the while."

The present generation may be interested in knowing what it cost to burn a good man, or several of them: —

"For three loads of wood fagots, 12s.
"Item, one load of furze fagots, 3s. 4d.
"For the carriage of these four loads, 2s.
"Item, A post, 1s. 4d.

"Item, Two chains, 3s. 4d.
"Item, Two staples, 6d.
"Item, Four laborers, 2s. 8d.
"Total cost of burning Ridley and Latimer, 1 pound, 5s. 2d."

The cost of burning Cranmer was eleven shillings, four pence.

Elizabeth ordered a "mild and gentle, not rigorous reformation" of the university. She, who disprized "logical conclusions," and who always steered a middle course, counseled the doctors to be moderate in their Protestantism. It was during her reign that Oxford received its best gift, the Bodleian Library, which is now so rich in manuscripts, and which is so dear to all the lovers of lore.

But, in another particular, Elizabeth's time was less benignant. The heaviest blow dealt to Oxford came from her favorite, the Earl of Leicester, whose chancellorship has been referred to. He it was who shut the gates of that place of learning in the face of all who would not subscribe to the Thirty-nine Articles and to the Act of Supremacy. This proscription, which was directed solely against Catholics, afterwards came to include Puritans and Wesleyans; in fact, all forms of dissent. Oxford thus contracted into a Church of England institution, resembling in some respects a theological seminary, and ceased to be a university. The splendid title then lost was not regained until the present century, when, in these knowing and denying days, the walls of a Unitarian college are rearing themselves in the very shadows of old and frowning ecclesiastical halls.

History has dealt hardly with Leicester's name in other matters, and less justly. He is linked forever, and in an ignoble way, with the fate of Amy Robsart, who lived and died at Cumnor Hall, three miles southeast of Oxford. Romance would seem to be alien to the home of monasticism, and yet Scott's unfortunate heroine is buried in the university church. A very illegible manuscript in the Bodleian gives an account of her funeral. There was a great procession. "The pore men and women in gownes . . . the universities, two and two together accordinge to the degres of the colleges, and before every house ther officers with their staves . . . the quere in surplesses singinge, and after them the minestar ... the corpes borne by eight yoemen for the way was farre." The body was placed on the hearse, and on "eche syde of the hersse stod two gentlemen holdinge the banneroles, and at the feet stood he that held the great banner."[1]

Scott, we are assured, was misled by the mistake of the nervous Doctor Babbington, who preached the funeral sermon. Thrice did he recommend to men's memory that virtuous lady so pitifully "murdered," instead of saying so pitifully "slain,"—a difference somewhat occult. Later investigations show that the marriage of Amy Robsart and Robert Dudley was not secret, but was conducted in the presence of Edward VI. She died in 1560, although Scott represents her as an inmate of Kenilworth, during Elizabeth's visit, fifteen years later. It appears also that at her death Robert Dudley persistently demanded an inquest; that a jury was impaneled, every man of whom was a stranger to him, and that they rendered a verdict of accidental death.

The exterior of St. Mary's Church, the tomb

Moore's *Historical Handbook*, p. 47.

of Amy Robsart, is richly ornamented, and there arises a pinnacled spire which is a marvel of airiness and grace. In the Middle Ages, this edifice had served as the great hall of the university, as its seat of justice, of legislation, of examination, and of worship. It fronts on High Street, a thoroughfare said to be one of the finest in Great Britain. Wordsworth speaks of the "streamlike windings of that glorious street," which, lined with stately colleges, is terminated in Magdalen bridge, a beautiful stone structure that spans the Cherwell. Over this bridge came the coaches from London in the olden days, laden with students, who greeted their Alma Mater with the musical post-horn. At the end of the bridge, Magdalen tower shoots up, a lofty structure, famous for the beauty of its proportions, and under it nestles Magdalen College, founded in the fifteenth century by William of Waynflete, Bishop of Winchester, and Lord High Chancellor.

The encompassing gardens form a fit setting for this gem; and they are famous as well, for here, beneath the elms, Addison was "steeping himself in the Latin poets and tagging

Latin verses" during ten years. His "walk" is probably the most observed spot in Oxford. It is easy to understand the inspiration which he drew from the place. The gardens from his time have been inclosed with a defensive wall. Part of them are used as a deer park now. What with the flowing waters, the ancient trees, the shaded walks, the cool cloisters, the curious quadrangles, and the quaint carvings, it is not surprising that the sweet serenity of the college of "Seinte Marie Maugdalene" should be reflected in the character and writings of the great essayist.

In 1649, the head of Magdalen College invited Cromwell and Fairfax to dine with him; and it is said that, in return for this hospitality, his guests appropriated the organ in the chapel, and had it conveyed to Hampton Court, and that their followers broke the painted glass out of the windows, and trampled it under foot. The Puritans had a fashion of whitewashing the walls of all chapels that were decorated. They knew no more and cared no more about art than Biagio, who remonstrated with Paul III. concerning Michael Angelo's picture of the Last

Judgment. He complained that the nudity of the figures was inappropriate to the Sistine Chapel. Michael Angelo, the "baptized Phidias," took his revenge by putting Biagio in hell, and by giving him the ears of an ass; and there he is to this day. Fortunate Puritan Fathers!

It was the Cavaliers, however, and not the Roundheads, who played havoc with Oxford. When King Charles occupied the town, they used the cloisters and schools as magazines and granaries, and the colleges as barracks. The functions of the university were practically suspended. With the supremacy of the Puritans, Cromwell became chancellor of the university, and, despite the ungracious act here before mentioned, he proved to be a kindly patron of learning, he himself having been a student at Cambridge. There was, of course, the usual visitation, which was followed, at the Restoration, by another.

After the revolution, as before, royalty sojourned at Oxford; but more frequently in the earlier centuries, when Woodstock was a royal palace. The comings of the sovereigns were always festal occasions. Anthony Wood gravely informs us that, with the visit of James I. and his court in 1603, the students became dissipated, and that there was much drunkenness, a statement calculated to leave upon the unguarded mind the inference that prior to that time Oxford had been very exemplary indeed. It is difficult to believe so well of its early days. Certainly the traditions are against it, if we are to accept as descriptive a bacchanalian note uttered in the long ago by Walter Mapes, Archdeacon of Oxford. The verses, delightfully paraphrased by Leigh Hunt, run in this wise: —

> "Mihi est propositum in taberna mori,
>   Vinum sit appositum morientis ori,
>   Ut dicant, cum venerint angelorum chori;
>   'Deus sit propitius huic potatori.'
>
> "Poculis accendentur animi lucerna;
>   Cor inbutum nectare volat ad superna;
>   Mihi sapit dulcius vinum in taberna,
>   Quam quod aqua miscuit præsulis pincerna.
>
> "Suum cuique proprium dat natura munus,
>   Ego nunquam potui scribere jejunus;
>   Ne jejunum vincere posset puer unus;
>   Sitim et jejunium odi tanquam funus.

"Tales versus facio quale vinum bibo,
  Non possum scribere nisi sumpto cibo ;
  Nihil valet penitus quod jejunus scribo,
  Nasonem post calices facile præibo.

"Mihi nunquam spiritus prophetiæ datur,
  Nisi cum fuerit venter bene satur ;
  Cum in acre cerebri Bacchus dominatur,
  In me Phœbus irruit ac miranda fatur."

"I devise to end my days — in a tavern drinking;
May some Christian hold for me — the glass when I am shrinking;
That the cherubim may cry — when they see me sinking,
God be merciful to a soul — of this gentleman's way of thinking.

"A glass of wine amazingly — enlighteneth one's internals;
'T is wings bedewed with nectar — that fly up to supernals;
Bottles cracked in taverns — have much the sweeter kernels,
Than the sups allowed to us — in the college journals.

"Every one by nature hath — a mould which he was cast in:
I happen to be one of those — who never could write fasting;
By a single little boy — I should be surpass'd in
Writing so: I 'd just as lief — be buried, tomb'd and grass'd in.

"Every one by nature hath — a gift, too, a dotation;
I, when I make verses, — do get the inspiration
Of the very best wine — that comes into the nation;
It maketh sermons to abound — for edification.

"Just as liquor floweth good — floweth forth my lay so;
But I must moreover eat — or I could not say so;
Nought it availeth inwardly — should I write all day so;
But with God's grace after meat — I beat Ovidius Naso.

"Neither is there given to me — prophetic animation,
Unless when I have eat and drank — yea, ev'n to saturation
Then in my upper story — hath Bacchus domination,
And Phœbus rusheth into me — and beggareth all relation."

It was a merry Oxford indeed, then and afterwards; and good stories of its conviviality are not lacking. Humphrey Prideaux, an annalist of the university, and contemporary of Anthony Wood, tells us that there was once "a dingy, horrid, scandalous ale-house" over against Balliol College, where a "hellish liquor cald ale" was sold, for which the fellows of Balliol had a liking. Thomas Good, master of Balliol, protested vigorously against this "perpetuall bubbeing;" and was informed by one who was "not willing soe tamely to be preached out of his beloved liquor," that the "vice-chancellor's men also drink ale at the Split Crow. . . . The old man being nonplussed with this reply immediately packeth off to the vice-chancelour, who . . . was an old lover of ale himselfe, and who answered him roughly, that there was noe hurt in ale." Thereupon the master of Balliol returned to his college, called the fellows together again, and told them that as he had been assured that there was no hurt in ale, they all might now be "sots by authority."

The visits of Charles II. to Oxford did not promote the decorum of university life, although they may have strengthened the authority of the Crown. After the discovery of the Rye House plot (1683), the university, in an extraordinary fit of flunkeyism, decreed "against certain pernicious books and damnable doctrines destructive to the sacred persons of Princes, their State and Government, and of all Human Society." The decree recited twenty-seven propositions as heretical, and condemned the books which contained and expounded them "to be publicly burnt by the hand of our marshal in the court of our schools." An examination of some of the propositions, as set out in the decree, discloses that it was the books and not the doctrines which were destroyed in the university bonfire.

The first three propositions are as follows:—

"The 1st proposition. All civil authority is derived originally from the people.

"2. There is a mutual compact, tacit or express, between a prince and his subjects, that if he perform not his duty, they are discharged from theirs.

"3. That if lawful governors become tyrants, or govern otherwise than by the laws of God and man they ought to do, they forfeit the right they had unto their government. Lex Rex; Buchanan, de Jure Regni; Vindiciæ contra tyrannos; Bellarmine, de Conciliis, de Pontifice; Milton; Goodwin; Baxter; H. C."

In solemn reprobation of these "false, seditious, and impious" propositions, the university proclaimed the doctrine of Divine Right, and enjoined passive obedience upon all persons subject to its authority. It was soon to taste the fruits of this servility.

James II. came to Oxford in an ugly mood. Although he had no legal right to name the heads of colleges, he endeavored personally to coerce Magdalen College into accepting a candidate of his choice. His first nominee, a papist, was rejected by the fellows as unfit to hold the office, and another man was elected. James's second nominee, the Bishop of Oxford, was installed by force after the president and twenty-five fellows had been ejected. At one time William Penn visited Oxford as a mediator between the king and the belligerent institution. The founder of Pennsylvania was not unknown to the university, whence he had been expelled long before for participation in the "surplice riot." It seems that he was enrolled in Christ Church during the Protectorate, and that after the Restoration, when some students made their appearance for the first time in white surplices, he and others fell upon them zealously, and stripped them of the hated garments. Christ Church, or Cardinal College, Penn's sometime collegiate home, is the most splendid foundation in Oxford. Founded by Wolsey, it was completed by Henry VIII., who diverted to its maintenance the revenues of twenty-two priories and convents (themselves suppressed). It occupies ground sacred in pietistic tradition. Here rest (supposedly) the bones of St. Frideswide, a maiden of the eighth century, who devoted herself to a monastic life. Her father built for her upon this spot a conventual church, in the tower of which a number of fugitive Jews and

Danes were burned shortly after the Danish invasion. In architecture Christ Church is unsurpassed. The present college consists of four quadrangles, three of them small, and one very large and magnificent. The gateway is surmounted by a tower (designed by Sir Christopher Wren, a son of Oxford), which contains the "Great Tom" bell, the thirty-first in size of the world. Before it was recast in 1680, it bore the following inscription, which attests the resonance of the tone and the soundness of the metal:—

"In Thomæ laude resono Bim Bom sine fraude."

A dean of Christ Church of the seventeenth century extolled the bells of his college in the following verse:—

"Hark! the bonny Christ Church bells,—
1, 2, 3, 4, 5, 6,—
They sound so wondrous great, so woundy sweet,
As they trowl so merrily, merrily.
Oh! the first and second bell,
That every day, at four and ten, cry,
'Come, come, come, come to prayers!'
And the Verger troops before the Dean,
Tinkle, tinkle, ting, goes the small bell at nine,

> To call the bearers home;
> But the devil a man
> Will leave his can
> Till he hears the mighty Tom."

Christ Church is built of stone, as, indeed, are all the colleges of Oxford, save one. It remained for the nineteenth century to erect a structure of red and yellow brick. The beauties of Christ Church are many. There is a noble Gothic fane, and a refectory whose oak roof is a wonder. There are fretted stone ceilings and graceful springing columns. But all these are for the pencil. Christ Church has a great human interest, since it boasts many illustrious names. Among these may be mentioned rare Ben Jonson, Sir Philip Sidney, and Richard Hakluyt, the stay-at-home traveler, "whose diction," says Lowell, "we should be glad to buy back from desuetude at any cost."

In the hall (the seat of many parliaments) are some noted portraits, and among them one, by Kneller, of John Locke, who held a scholarship here for a number of years. Locke was expelled at the instigation of the crown, after the Convocation had issued the celebrated decree of 1683.

Owing to his intimacy with the Earl of Shaftesbury, and to his retired if not secretive habits, he was accused of complicity in plots against the government of Charles II. We can only hope that the charge was true. If Christ Church had an intellectual reformer in John Locke, it had an emotional one in John Wesley. After graduation Wesley was elected a Fellow of Lincoln College, and was appointed Greek lecturer. His range of study included the classics, logic, ethics, mathematics, Hebrew, Arabic, metaphysics, natural philosophy, rhetoric, poetry, and divinity. Methodism originated in a club of which he, his brother Charles, and Whitefield were members, and who were nicknamed by the Oxonians, Bible Bigots, Bible Moths, Holy Club, and, at last, Methodists. Whitefield, in his devotional ecstasies, would lie on the ground in Christ Church, on winter nights, until he would almost perish from cold. John Wesley mixed a little in politics. Before going to America, he preached in St. Mary's Church a sermon that "smacked of treason," and concerning which his brother Charles said: "My brother has been mauled, and threatened more, for his Jacobite sermon in St. Mary's. But he was wise enough to get the vice-chancellor to read and approve it before he preached it, and may therefore bid Wadham, Exeter, and Christ Church do their worst," which, it must be said, the colleges in Oxford oftentimes did. At one time Wesley thought he was going to die, and so composed his own epitaph : " Here lieth the body of John Wesley, a brand plucked out of the burning, who died of a consumption in the fifty-first year of his age, not leaving, after his debts are paid, ten pounds behind him, praying God to be merciful to me, an unprofitable servant."

He recovered, and lived thirty-seven years after, and evidently to some purpose. The Methodist Club of fifteen members has expanded into a church of twenty-five millions. Methodism also possessed political consequence. The eloquence of Wesley and Whitefield attracted the first great public meetings held in England. It was the initial exercise of the art of popular persuasion. These novel gatherings taught the multitude their right to assemble, and, it may be, discovered to them their equality of condition, their community of interest, and the enormous power which lay stored in them as "the people."[1] Contemporary with Wesley was Berkeley, who is buried in Christ Church Cathedral, and Butler, who studied in Oriel College. If the deistic movement in England may be said to owe its origin to Locke, and therefore to Christ Church, the anti-deistic movement may also, in a sense, be ascribed to Oriel. In the present century, Oriel was the scene of yet another religious revival, — the "Oxford Movement." Though Catholic in its tendencies, Tractarianism, Puseyism, or Newmanism, as it was differently called, had a vastly invigorating effect upon the Established Church. "Forty years ago," says Matthew Arnold, "when I was an undergraduate at Oxford, voices were in the air there which haunt my memory still. . . . He (Newman) was in the very prime of life; he was close at hand to us at Oxford; he was preaching in St. Mary's pulpit every Sunday; he seemed about to transform and to renew what was for us the most national and natural institution in the world, the Church of England. Who could resist the charm of that spiritual apparition,

---

[1] Henry Jephson, *The Platform: Its Rise and Progress*, p. 4.

gliding in the dim afternoon light through the aisles of St. Mary's, rising into the pulpit, and then, in the most entrancing of voices, breaking the silence with words and thoughts which were a religious music,— subtile, sweet, mournful? I seem to hear him still, saying : ' After the fever of life, after wearinesses and sicknesses, fightings and despondings, languor and fretfulness, struggling and succeeding ; after all the changes and chances of this troubled, unhealthy state,— at length comes death, at length the white throne of God, at length the beatific vision.' "

Oxford was notoriously high church, and the Neo-Catholic revival more nearly accorded with the traditions of the place than any other movement of its later history. Newman severed his connection with the university by resignation, faring better in this respect than some of his gifted predecessors. Oxford had a way of expelling its geniuses, as we have seen. Gibbon went to Magdalen College "with a stock of information which might have puzzled a doctor, and a degree of ignorance of which a school-boy might be ashamed." The fourteen months which he spent there were, he said, the most idle and unprofitable of his whole life. Perhaps the mind of the great historian — the conspicuous infidel of his day — was stirred uneasily, in after years, by the recollection that he had been expelled from Oxford for joining the Catholic Church. Other sons, such as Dr. Johnson, of Pembroke, whose experiences, though different, were less pleasant, had kindlier memories of the place. In the present century, the university sent adrift the poet Shelley, one of the marked individualities of his time, and the "Pagan" Landor. De Quincey (who, by the way, first tasted opium in his second year at Oxford) explains that Shelley was expelled, not for compiling and publishing an atheistical or deistical pamphlet, but for his ostentation in sending a copy of the pamphlet to each of the dons, which was accounted a breach of discipline. Walter Savage Landor was dismissed from Trinity College for playfully emptying the contents of a double-barreled shotgun into the windows of a man living upon the opposite side of the quadrangle, of whose political opinions he did not approve. Although the shutters were closed, and no bodily damage was done, the university failed utterly to discover in this impulsive and highly original act the distinctive poetic temperament, and so Landor was "sent down," as the phrase runs.

The university was more lenient in the last half of the last century, when it would forgive almost anything but religious apostasy. Tutors were listless, and proctorial authority limp. "The fellows of Magdalen," says Gibbon, "were decent, easy men, who supinely enjoyed the gifts of the founder. . . . From the toil of reading, or thinking, or writing, they had absolved their consciences." This was during one of the periods of depression which marked the university life from time to time, and which may be partly explained by the fact that for centuries the university had been subjected to ecclesiastical espionage. It had lost in vitality when its democratic constitution was destroyed by Leicester and Laud. It was swallowed up by the colleges, which were themselves little more than adjuncts of the Established Church.

Independence, the essential attribute of the ideal university, was lacking. A temple of learning should be supported neither by the church nor by the state; and its benefactions should not be the expressions of mental caprice. Those colleges in Oxford have prospered most whose fellowships have been freest. Of these may be mentioned Balliol College, noted for its high scholarship. The rolls of Balliol are illuminated by illustrious names such as those of Adam Smith, who, like Locke, created a science, and of Southey, and of Swinburne. Its present master is B. Jowett, the Regius professor of Greek, whose delightful translations have made Plato the familiar of the English reading world. With the successive creation of professorships the university has emerged and again taken form. It is known for ripe erudition, and has included among its instructors of recent years Liddell, Stubbs, Max Müller, Earle, Maine, Ruskin, John Richard Green, Goldwin Smith, Freeman, Froude, Bryce, Thorold Rogers, H. Morse Stephens, and W. R. Morfill, not to mention a host of others. Six schools of honors have been established: theology, natural science, jurisprudence, mathematics, modern history, and *literæ humaniores*; the examination system has been modified and perfected; and all religious tests have been abolished. Once more the university is hospitable to men and thought.

Any sketch of Oxford, however fragmentary, would imply some reference to Cambridge, the twin English university. The two institutions are correlatives. They were born about the same time, and they have run nearly parallel lives. The rivalry between them has been generous, and has produced more than one neat epigram. The most celebrated of these grew out of the persistent Jacobitism of Oxford, lasting even to the time of George I. With the incoming of the Hanoverian dynasty, Tory Oxford was restive and openly favored the Pretender. The new king sent a troop of horse there to keep the peace, and at the same time he gave a splendid library to Cambridge. This evoked the following Oxford verse: —

> "The king observing, with judicious eyes,
> The state of both his universities,
> To Oxford sent a troop of horse; and why?
> That learned body wanted loyalty;
> To Cambridge books he sent, as well discerning
> How much that loyal body wanted learning."

A Cambridge graduate thereupon made this reply, which Dr. Johnson pronounced to be one of the best extemporaneous productions he had ever met with.

> "The king to Oxford sent a troop of horse,
> For Tories own no argument but force;
> With equal skill to Cambridge books he sent,
> For Whigs admit no force but argument."

The two universities are absolutely more efficient in the present than they were in the past, but they are relatively less important. Outside of them there are a thousand and one educational influences which did not exist in the Middle Ages. Then, they were the eyes of England, peopling

> "The hollow dark like burning stars."

Now they seem less brilliant only because they have helped to usher in the day.

SOME POPULAR OBJECTIONS TO CIVIL SERVICE REFORM.

SOME POPULAR OBJECTIONS TO CIVIL SERVICE REFORM.[1]

"You gentlemen never weary of telling us that we are fallen upon degenerate days; that during the first forty years of our government, before we lapsed from our sinless state, officials were removed only for cause, and incumbents held on good behavior; in other words, that civil service reform prevailed in all its purity. Now, it is philosophical generalization, founded on broad experience, that revolutions do not go backwards. Heed it, gentlemen, heed it! The revolution of 1820–29 is an accomplished fact. It is here to stay, for then did the people come

---

[1] Such of these objections as are taken from the records of Congress are indicated by marginal notes and are quoted literally. The others — which reflect current lay discussion of the newspaper and the street — are repeated substantially, but not formally.

into their own. The present status has endured for a half century; civil service reform is ancient history. You are chasing moonbeams."

The fatalist intrenches himself in platitude, and warns reason beyond speaking distance. With him, what is must forever be; what has been and is not will never be. And thus is the controversy closed.

He forgets that much that is done remains to be undone; that political progress is mostly negative, consisting mainly in the repeal of bad laws or in the abolition of evil customs. In this sense history is reversed every day, and the process will continue, so long as legislation is experimental, and legislators are supine. It is true that some things in political history may be regarded as settled. But this can be predicated only of those changes which are based upon the immutable principles of right. The introduction of the spoils system into the administrative branch of the American government is not of these. That system is at war with equality, freedom, justice, and a wise economy, and is already a doomed thing fighting extinction. Its establishment was in no sense a popular revolution, but was the work of a self-willed man of stubborn and tyrannical nature, who had enemies to punish, and debts to pay. He overrode a vehement opposition, disregarding the protest and sage prediction of the great statesmen of his time. He wielded a power that was arbitrary; his caprice was law, his rule was a reign. If he wished to do a thing, it was enough that it seemed good to him to do it. His idea of government was a personal one solely. Every public official was a private servitor, who must take the oath of allegiance and do homage to his chief. In his view, no man could honestly disagree with him. He was always right; his opponents were hopelessly and criminally wrong. Here was a fit man to establish the spoils system, to explore the Constitution for latent executive powers, to attach to the person of the President the high prerogatives of a monarch. That the king is the fountain of honor, office, and privilege is the theory of the English state; that the civil service of the United States is a perquisite of the presidency was the theory of General Jackson.

It is needless to say that the American commonwealth was not founded upon any such doctrine. Jackson's interpretation of the Constitution was a gross perversion of the intent and meaning of that instrument. This was to be a government of laws, not of men; and so far as the prescience of its framers availed it was made so. The liberties of the people were not to be left to individual scruple, but were to be secured by specific inhibitions upon the governmental agencies. Three departments were organized severally to make, execute, and interpret the laws, and each was to act as a check upon the other. With the adoption of the first ten amendments to the Constitution, it was thought that every avenue of attack upon popular rights had been closed. But the power of construction is greater than that of legislation. The intention of the lawgiver is determined, not by himself, but by some other who construes the law; and with that other interpretation is purely a subjective matter. Madison held that "the wanton removal of meritorious officers" was an impeachable offense. But Jackson swore to defend and to protect the Constitution as he understood it, and not as Madison, one of its framers, conceived it. Regarding the right of removal the instrument itself is silent, except as it provides impeachment for high crimes and misdemeanors. When, therefore, Jackson organized the civil service into a gigantic political machine, proscribing office-holders because of his personal enmity to them, or because of their political affiliations, it cannot be said that he violated any specific provision of the Constitution. That such action was an usurpation of authority and a wanton betrayal of trust needs no verbal emphasis. With equal propriety and moral justification, he might have used those other coördinate branches of the executive department, the army and navy, to perpetuate himself and his party in power. This he did not attempt to do. Perhaps he did not need their aid. At any rate, after securing his own reëlection and after naming his successor, his ambition rested, — fortunately for the country. But what he did, he did thoroughly. The system of political brigandage inaugurated by him has subsisted even unto this day, although it is now upon the verge of dissolution. Its end is written and sealed. This last is the work of those who are grown weary of the spoliation of office, — of those who are jealous of the encroachments of the Executive, and who would tie the hands of that functionary for all time to come. With them, it is not a question whether a clerk holds his office for four years or for fifteen years. They are determined that the great army of the civil service shall not be used by any man or by any set of men for purposes of personal or partisan aggrandizement; that the freedom of elections shall not be assailed by an intriguing, corrupt, and organized official force; that presidential contests shall not be tumults threatening anarchy. Hereafter there will be no " prizes of victory," no carnival of spoil. Place-holders will attend to the business for which they are paid to attend; fitness will be the essential of appointment, not the accident and the incident. This is the popular revolution that is moving forward irresistibly, that is coming to stay. A law has been enacted which, though partial in its effects, is capable of large extension by the President alone, without further action on the part of Congress. This measure leaves the power of removal for all except partisan reasons untouched. By regulating the method of appointment, it takes away the temptation to the abuse of that discretion. It is not a revival of a faded statute, nor has it its counterpart in early legislation. It is a new ordering of things; practically, a reversal of procedure. Although there was no statutory restriction upon the manner of appointment and removal, during the first forty years of the republic, nevertheless the power of removal was controlled by an unwritten law, which depended for its enforcement upon mental sanctions.[1] But this was a frail dyke with which to withstand the pressure of a hungry and inflowing sea, and it was only a question of time until it should be swept away. That Congress did not strengthen it by positive legislation is to be deplored. But the omission is explicable. At the time of the formation of our government no law was deemed necessary. The civil service numbered but two thousand persons; to-day it numbers two hundred thousand, and not many decades hence it will increase to a half million. Again, Con-

[1] The sum of the removals from 1789 to 1829 was seventy-three. John Quincy Adams displaced but two persons during four years. His successor, Andrew Jackson, removed seven hundred persons during one year.

gress had absolute faith in the Executive. All Presidents would be Washingtons, patient and moderate, patriotic rather than partisan. So highly was the first President esteemed that that body waived its consent to the removal of those officers whose appointment required their approval. Of course they did not contemplate the capricious exercise of this power ; the causeless removal of an official being to them an unthinkable proposition. But events outran prevision, and in the course of years not only did a Jackson appear, but Congress itself ceased to desire to protect the service. Such legislative changes as were made subserved a private and not a public interest. The immense patronage which was controlled by the Chief Executive, either directly by commission, or indirectly through the heads of departments, came to be administered for the benefit of the representative politicians as well as of himself. This step was gained partly through a recognition by the President of the eminent utility of sub-allotment for personal purposes, and partly, in the failure of that persuasion, through the exercise of such coercive power as could be wielded by the Senate in confirmation, and by both houses in the passage of acts regulating the term and tenure of office. Gradually, out of the chaotic scramble for spoil, there was evolved a system of distribution which was founded upon hoary precedent, and which, in nice precision and in perfection of detail, lacked nothing of a scientific character. The whole country was staked out into districts, as many in number as there were Congressmen. After a conquest, the enemy were driven from their holdings, and the victors took possession of the glebe. But the estates thus granted were made conditional upon the performing of certain services or upon the rendering of certain tribute. Each tenant held of some feudal superior, and all held, mediately or immediately, of the lord paramount, the President. The governmental offices scattered everywhere were so many baronial strongholds, and were filled with retainers who were chosen for their fighting qualities.

The chief duty of these men was to check uprisings and to keep the people in subjection. Their places depended upon the faithful discharge of it. In other words, the civil service was a graded vassalage of a militant character. All offices were the private property of the head of the state, and were dispensed by royal favor. What is this but feudalism in new clothes, or, rather, the garbed skeleton thereof? By some fantastic jugglery, this mocking semblance of a dead and buried past has become a stalking figure in a new and progressive civilization. Verily has a revolution gone backwards, if it be not promptly relegated to the glass case of antiquities, there to remain as a curiosity for posterity to stare at.

The spoils system should have perished a quarter of a century ago, in the cataclysm which destroyed that other relic of feudalism, slavery. They were twin evils, and were ever unfailing allies; and when the time shall come to write the history of public opinion in America during the nineteenth century, they will be classed together. John Morley says: "Nobody has yet traced out the full effect upon the national character of the Americans of all those years of conscious complicity in slavery, after the immorality and iniquity of slavery had become clear to the inner conscience of the very men who ignobly sanctioned the mobbing of the Abolitionists." [1]

Adherence to the letter of a contract which was "a covenant with death and an agreement with hell" was due partly to an unfaltering instinct of Union. But many were influenced by motives less worthy. Before the war the fidelity of most Northern politicians to the South was a degrading sycophancy. Eager and grateful for the crumbs which fell from the Southern table, and despairing of obtaining those crumbs elsewhere, they suffered themselves to become the supple tools of the slave power. These "Swiss guards of slavery fighting for pay" were a race of place-hunters, with whom office was the end, not the means, and whose statesmanship, like that of the Augustan Senate, consisted in justifying personal flattery by speculative principles of servitude. They steadily prostituted principle to preferment, and came near involving this country in irretrievable ruin.

But the age of compromise — the era of "bigotry with a doubt" and of "persecution without

[1] Harriet Martineau, *Critical Miscellanies*, p. 268.

a creed" — was succeeded by the age of blood and iron. The war was an ethical education; like a great storm, it purified the air. After it was over the people began to see more clearly and more truly; they learned to view things "in the visual angle of the absolute principle."

Before this keener vision the spoils system, a long-established practice claiming charter by prescription, has been called upon to justify itself. Until recently, the people of this country supposed that traffic in place, the unceasing clamor for office, the sack and pillage of the government by the dominant party, were a necessary part of democratic institutions. Many politicians, with selfish purposes to subserve, were interested in enforcing this view. To the principle that the majority must rule they added the corollary that all the offices are essential to that rule. They further inculcated the idea that every national election is a battle of enemies, instead of an amicable contest of friends, whose interests are the same, and "who disagree not except in opinion."

It must be confessed that during the Rebellion, when the North was divided between the war party and the peace party, there was some foundation for this doctrine. He who was not with you was against you. But the intense partisanism engendered by that strife is relaxing into an amiable toleration. Happily, party fealty is not always to be a test of patriotism. The government is not the property of faction, and the minority have rights which must be respected. " Væ victis " is no longer the slogan of the fight. If civil service reform has not made that progress which idealists expect, — conquering all on the instant, — let it be remembered that the growth of moral movements is necessarily slow, especially in a democracy, where, it is scarcely hyperbole to say, the last man must be convinced. It is none the less sure, however, for "one man in the right becomes a majority," and the American people mean to do right when they know where the right lies.

II.

"I believe this commission to be undemocratic. I believe that it favors certain voters in this country at the expense of other voters, and

I know that if the rulings of the civil service commission were applied to the members of this House not seven eighths of the members would ever reach the floor again. [Laughter.] Now, sir, believing this to be undemocratic, and believing that it is in violation of the fundamental principles of the government, I move to strike out the whole section, and hope that it will be agreed to." [1]

To apply the rules of the merit system to the members of Congress would be a cruelty indeed, and is altogether a harrowing suggestion. But it is beside the point. If civil service reform be undemocratic, and if it violate the fundamental principles of our government, the motion made in the House of Representatives to strike out the appropriation to the commission should have prevailed. As a matter of fact, it was overwhelmingly defeated by a vote of twenty-five to one hundred and thirty-eight. This would appear to be decisive. It is evident, however, from the discussion that preceded the calling of the yeas and nays, that the scope

---

[1] Mr. Cummings, *Proceedings of the House of Representatives*, December 19, 1888.

and object of civil service reform are still profoundly misunderstood by some Congressmen, and inferentially by their constituencies. A restatement may therefore serve a useful purpose:—

The doctrine of civil service reform as applied to the subordinate, clerical, or purely ministerial offices of the government is based upon the following self-evident propositions: that offices are created to fulfill certain necessary functions involved in the routine of government, and not to give some men a place; that offices are supported by non-partisan taxation; that taxation is an evil, and therefore the public service should be as efficient and economical as possible; that offices are public and not private property, and administration is a trust, not an ownership; that in a republic something less arbitrary than favoritism shall govern appointment and removal; that men shall be appointed solely on the ground of merit, and not in payment of personal debt; that an examination is the fairest means of ascertaining the qualifications of an appointee, because it insures that a clerk shall know how to write, a book-keeper how to keep books, and a gauger how to gauge; that such examination shall be competitive and open to all, not being confined to the members of any one political party; that a class system is opposed to the spirit of our institutions, and therefore offices should not be the vested property of ward-workers and political henchmen, to the total and absolute exclusion of the great body of the common people; that an office-holder is a citizen of the United States, and is entitled to the rights and privileges attaching to such citizenship; that neither the President nor any other executive officer has the right to proscribe such office-holder, remove him from place, or threaten his subsistence on account of his politics; that such procedure is un-American; that tenure of office should not be dependent upon the degradation of manhood and the prostitution of political opinion; that the practice of the President and his cabinet in changing two hundred thousand office-holders at will, for causes unconnected with good administration, is dangerous and despotic, and should be restrained; that under the present system these office-holders constitute a great standing army of paid servitors, ever ready to do the bidding of their patrons, to the perversion of the public will, and are a menace to good government; that political assessments, if paid unwillingly, are an extortion and a direct theft from the office-holder, and, if paid willingly, are generally a brokerage commission for appointment, or a bribe to the appointing power for continuance in place; that if salaries are so large that assessments can be endured without inconvenience, such salaries should be cut down to a saving of the people's money; that promises of appointment to office made, whether definitely or indefinitely, work a corruption of public opinion; that the enormous bribe of two hundred thousand offices, offered as a reward for party work, tends to obscure the real issues of politics, encourages the sacrifice of principle to selfish personal gain, and induces a laxity of political morals; that a "clean sweep" of the offices demoralizes the public service, and is the direct and indirect source of great financial loss; that skill in the manipulation of a caucus and in the packing of a primary is not presumptive evidence of capacity for the performance of official duties; that the Constitution of the United States contemplates the election of a Congressman as a legislator, and not as a patronage-monger; that such patronage is a burden to every honest, conscientious, and able Congressman, compels the neglect of his proper duties, creates petty factional disputes and wrangles among his constituents, and often defeats the reëlection of a trustworthy servant of honorable record ; that the statesman is thus rapidly becoming an extinct species, being succeeded by the politician, and the consequent loss inflicted on the people through crude and unwise legislation is incalculable ; that the fear of losing the spoils of office is paralyzing the legislative branch of the government, makes cowards of political parties, and is the enemy of progress ; that the retention of the vast patronage of two hundred thousand offices is becoming of more concern than the triumph of principle ; that the mania for place-hunting is increasing ; that the clamor of spoilsmen compels the creation of sinecures, thereby increasing the taxes; and finally, that all the evils here before enumerated are growing with the multiplication of offices, and will ultimately, unless checked by a comprehensive and decisive enactment, undermine and overthrow the institutions of our country.

Such is an imperfect outline of the doctrine of civil service reform and of the abuses it is designed to remedy. By this showing, is it not the spoils system which is "undemocratic," and which "favors certain voters of this country at the expense of other voters?" What, to repeat, can be less democratic, less American, than persecution for opinion's sake? Yet this is the very essence of the spoils system, its guiding spirit and its crowning infamy. If this assertion need further explication, it may be found in a recital of what takes place in this country when one party succeeds another in the control of the government. The newly elected President goes (by deputy) through all the departments, and may be supposed to interview each clerk in a conversation of which the following is typical: —

President. Whom did you vote for at the last election?

Clerk. That does not concern you. I am an American citizen, and have the right to vote for whomsoever I please, without being subjected afterwards to a governmental inquisition by you or any other man.

President. I asked the question in conformity with a time-honored practice, and shall insist upon an answer.

Clerk. Very well; I will answer the question, not because of your menaces, but because I do not hold my political opinions covertly. I voted for your opponent.

President. Then you must vacate this office.

Clerk. If you can show that I have not performed my duties properly, or that I have neglected them for politics or for any other reason, I am willing to go.

President. I have not looked into that; it is immaterial, any way. I want your place for some one else.

Clerk. For one of your partisan "workers," perhaps, whose qualifications you have also not looked into?

President. Possibly.

Clerk. By what right do you proscribe me, then? You are merely a trustee; these offices do not belong to you.

President. You are the victim of an illusion.

These offices do belong to me. They are my personal patronage and plunder, to do with whatsoever I will. If you refuse to resign, I will remove you.

Clerk. Very well; I will yield the place as I would my purse to a highwayman who puts a pistol to my head. Nevertheless, I denounce your action as an outrage upon my rights as an American citizen.

If this conversation does not often take place actually as reported, its substance is at least tacitly understood. Generally the clerk stifles his protest and resigns, quietly submitting to a system that is an heritage of barbarism. Proscription of minor office-holders on account of political opinion is as completely indefensible as proscription on account of religious belief. It has no proper place in the United States. It is an anachronism, and belongs to the age of the crusades against the Catholics and the Jews.

III.

"Civil service reform is an English importation, upon which, unfortunately, there is no tariff. We broke with England and with her monarchical institutions a century ago, and set up a government of our own, — a democratic government. It supplies our needs, and stands as an example to mankind. Servile imitation of foreign polities is unworthy of our pride of race or nation."

Anglophobia is in the American blood. A common law, language, literature, and religion do not of necessity constitute the ties of sentiment. Although the American people are the heirs of all the ages, they do not like to be reminded of their obligations, nor to acknowledge an ancestry. They will not claim kinship even with Shakespeare. To them their history knows no perspective; in the discovery of a new and virgin world was the beginning of things. England is the traditional enemy, and all the pretty speeches made over London dinner-tables do not alter this fact in the least. This prejudice seems to be enduring, and any appeal made to it by politicians is generally successful.

Happily, in the present case, the retort is complete. The spoils system, with the stamp of feudalism upon it, was imported into this country from England, where it had obtained in the modern form for one hundred and forty years. It pervaded all departments of the English state, the army, the navy, and the church, as well as the civil service, attaining a growth which it has never known here. Offices were openly bought and sold, the purchaser acquiring a proprietary interest therein. Rotten boroughs were exposed for sale in the market, and members of Parliament were bribed to the support of the crown by sinecures, pensions, and money. At the time our government was founded, the spoils system was flourishing luxuriantly in England, and George III. found it a most serviceable instrument in enforcing his policy of persecution against the thirteen colonies. It is a pity that those gentlemen who claim the spoils system as peculiarly "American" should have forgotten this. It embarrasses their argument. *Per contra*, the merit system is a democratic institution, and its practical application to our civil service was coeval with the beginning of our government. That England should have been before us in embodying it in the form of law proves nothing more than the immense progress which has been made in that country toward popular institutions.

IV.

"The executive power of Great Britain is hereditary, and changes only at the death of the monarch. The administration, however, changes at will, and may change every week. Therefore, the idea of life tenure for executive officers is consistent with an executive for life. Therefore, an official class of lifelong tenure is consistent with monarchical and aristocratic government, which is peculiarly a government of classes. But it is not consistent with a democratic government and a short-lived executive where no class is recognized by law and all men are equal."[1]

It happens, unfortunately for the consistency of this argument, that in England, under the modern system of parliamentary government,

[1] Senator Vance, *Cong. Rec.*, vol. xvii. Part III. p. 2949.

the administration is the executive. The executive powers of the crown are obsolete, having passed to the prime minister and his cabinet. But these officials " change at will ; " they " may change every week." Consequently, tenure on good behavior — miscalled life tenure — is consistent with democratic government and a short-lived executive. If civil service reform is not adapted to the United States, where the President holds for four years, *a fortiori*, it is not adapted to England, where the tenure of the premier — the real executive — is the shortest and most precarious imaginable. Indeed, what we call civil service reform is the very life of parliamentary government. If, with every change of the ministry, a " clean sweep " of the offices should be made, the English civil service would soon be in a state of anarchy. Under such a system, rapid alternation in party control would totally disorganize the administrative machinery of the government, and would be a perpetual threat against the existence of the empire itself, — a thing of course not to be tolerated. The situation in England was logically reducible to this : either the spoils system must be abolished, or some one party must be continued in power indefinitely, which would mean the destruction of popular government. There could be no hesitation in choosing. The new democracy achieved a victory over feudalistic privilege that was complete and final.

Even apart from any political principle, the reform has vindicated itself. When the administrative departments ceased to be asylums for decayed gentry, and were thrown open to public competition, there was an improvement in the morale and efficiency of the service. Reorganization upon the basis of the merit system was extended even to India, where the duties of officials are of a most delicate and complicated character, involving, as they do, tactful relations with and control over two hundred millions of aliens.

But it has come to pass that civil service reform, which was denounced in England as "democratic," is opposed in the United States as representing exactly the opposite tendencies. "Aristocracy," "bureaucracy," and "insolence of office" are expressions as familiar as they are misleading. They deserve a brief consideration.

Aristocracy means the permanent exaltation of a few individual names. It implies great social dignity and distinction, and generally is based upon an hereditary succession of title and land. An aristocracy of department clerks and mail-carriers is an absurdity. However worthy such persons may be, they will have no more social distinction than clerks in business houses, whose tenure is the same as theirs. They possess neither title nor wealth, and are condemned to a routine of labor. The effect of service in a great government machine is to sink individuality, not to exalt it. The tens of thousands of school-teachers who are in the pay of every State do not constitute an aristocracy. In fact, they are rarely in the public view, and this for the reason that they are not " in politics." Fortunately, the spoils system has not been applied to our public schools. If, however, it were the practice to dismiss all the Republican school-teachers whenever a Democratic governor should be elected, and *vice versa*, without doubt we should be feelingly assured that any other tenure would seriously imperil our institutions.

Bureaucracy is another chimera. It cannot

exist where the heads of administration are constantly changing, where admission to the civil service is open to all, and where the removal of the unfit servant is expeditious and easy.

Insolence of office is an *a priori* argument. It has been pertinently said, in answer to it, that, at the time tenure on good behavior was superseded by Crawford's four-year law and by Jackson's régime, it was never urged by the innovators as a reason for the change that the manners of office-holders were contemptuous and overbearing. The objection is an afterthought. Of the insolence of bureaucracy and of the arrogance of aristocracy, the American people have had no experience under any official tenure, and are not likely to have.

A civil service becomes formidable to the liberties of a people only when it seeks to perpetuate itself by interfering with elections. Inasmuch as this purpose (to override the public will and to create a bureaucracy) is the very vice of the American spoils system, speculation as to what may be, under civil service reform, can be profitably postponed to an observation of what is.

The countless minor offices of the United

States are filled by a distinct class known as "professional politicians." These men live by politics, receiving place as reward for political work. Their control of public office is monopolistic. Mr. Bryce estimates their number at two hundred thousand, but this is an underestimate. They constitute a guild, although they are not organized under formal articles of association. With them office-getting (or keeping in office) is an industry, and the fees and emoluments are accepted as payment for partisan services rather than for the exercise of official functions. The influence which the officeholders wield is altogether out of proportion to their numbers or to their intellectual attainments. But they possess this advantage over other classes, — they are unified and organized. They make the management of primaries and conventions the serious business of their lives, and acquire a skill and experience in "wire-pulling" which ordinary citizens cannot hope to cope with. The politics of the country is in the hands of these men. The people elect, but cannot nominate, being reduced to a choice of candidates selected by the politicians of opposing parties. These politicians dictate nominations, high and low, and afterwards foreclose a lien upon public place which they claim to have earned. All others, those who cannot show a certificate of this character, are excluded. The spoils system has been compared with a fairly conducted lottery, in which every one has an equal chance. But the analogy is loose. In all lotteries the prizes are limited to ticket-holders, and in the American political lottery the ticket-holders are few. The farmer, the shopkeeper, and the laborer generally have not the remotest chance of preferment, unless they can produce evidence of partisan work more or less technical or questionable. Of course the number who can offer such credentials is comparatively small. To begin with, all the members of the defeated political party (who, under our electoral system, constitute, as often as not, more than one half of the people) are rigidly debarred. Secondly, only that small contingent of the dominant party who have been of practical use to the candidates in convention and elsewhere receive any consideration whatever. The idea, therefore, that the offices are in the hands of the people is the shallowest of delusions. They are sold to the few for a price which the many are unwilling and are unable to pay. It is needless to say that, in this barter and sale of public place, the proper transaction of government business is lost sight of. Competency does not appoint an applicant, and cannot save an incumbent. Other motives of a mercenary or selfish character control in both cases. Office brokerage is a shameless and conspicuous fact, as the newspapers and the congressional debates daily attest. It is the great object of civil service reform to restore these offices to the people, and to overthrow the bastard aristocracy who have despoiled them. Those good citizens who are apprehensive of government by "official caste" need not strain their eyes to the future. They should look about them.

V.

"The political disqualification of office-holders is an invasion of their rights as American citizens."

Civil service reform, as embodied in the Pendleton Act of 1883, does not deny to an officeholder any rights which properly belong to him as a citizen of the United States; on the contrary, it restores to him those rights of which he has been deprived. It protects him against partisan discrimination by the appointing power; it protects his salary from assessment by his official superiors; it protects him against removal for refusing to render any political service. It restores to him the right to think for himself, and to register his opinion at the ballot-box, free from the espionage of the informer. In this wise the law protects him. But civil service reform, in its gross and scope, within the statute and without, looks to the protection of the people also. There are certain things which a citizen as a place-holder may not do. He may not use his official influence to coerce the political actions of his neighbor, to wit: he may not neglect the duties of his office to do a henchman's work; he may not pack primaries, manipulate conventions, collect and disburse election funds, corrupt the ballot-box, or tamper with the returns. Some of these things are forbidden by the federal and state criminal law; others not. But whether or not, any and all of them are grave breaches of his duty, both as a citizen and as an office-holder. Yet these are the things which, in varying kind and degree, many officials notoriously are doing. Is it necessary to characterize such partisan activity as a monstrous evil in a country where the triumph of right is a question of majority, or to justify the executive orders which have been issued to suppress it?

In England, more than a century ago, the interference of office-holders in elections assumed such proportions that the whole body of subordinates in the executive department were forbidden by law to vote for members of Parliament. In 1868, after the introduction of the merit system, this law was repealed, as being an unnecessary restriction. If a man procures an appointment on his deserts, and not through political influence, the obligations of appointee to patron do not exist, and the temptation to indulge in corrupt election practices disappears. The American doctrine of the relation of the office-holder to the body politic was set forth (albeit little to the immediate purpose) by

President Cleveland in an executive order issued July 14, 1886. In it he said : —

"Individual interest and activity in political affairs are by no means condemned. Officeholders are neither disfranchised nor forbidden the exercise of political privileges, but their privileges are not enlarged, nor is their duty to party increased to pernicious activity, by officeholding. A just discrimination in this regard between the things a citizen may properly do and the purposes for which a public office should not be used is easy, in the light of a correct appreciation of the relation between the people and those intrusted with official place, and the consideration of the necessity, under our form of government, of political action free from official coercion."

VI.

"Is a competitive examination the best or any test for official competency or efficiency? May not a man be eminently competent for official preferment, and not at all competent for a competitive examination?"[1]

---

[1] Senator Call, *Cong. Rec.*, vol. xiv. Part I. p. 498.

The system of competitive examination may not be perfectly adapted to ascertaining the comparative fitness of candidates for place; but it is the best that has been suggested, and it is infinitely better than a system in which fitness is scarcely considered at all.

It accomplishes, within the sphere to which it has been limited, the chief object of civil service reform, namely, the removal of the ministerial offices from the domain of partisan politics. It tends also to increase the efficiency and to decrease the cost of the civil service, — an important though secondary consideration. There are some kinds of officers who cannot well be chosen by competition: the fourth-class postmasters, for instance, who live in sparsely settled districts, and who may be appointed by one of several feasible plans that have been suggested, and the higher grade of officers, such as chiefs of bureaus, whose competency would be better assured if they should obtain their positions by promotion, based upon worth, fidelity, and long experience. As to the intermediate officers, the system of competitive examination works satisfactorily. The official duties are clearly defined, and it is an easy matter to test the qualifications of applicants. If it be urged that business men do not select their employees by this method, it may be replied that they always make searching verbal inquiries into the capacity of applicants, and that, in some instances, where large numbers of men are employed, rigid tests have been adopted. In fact, competition, in some form, is the unwritten law of the commercial world, it being a needful guarantee of the best service.

It is, of course, possible that a man may be "eminently competent for official preferment, and not at all competent for a competitive examination;" but the chances are greatly against it, if the examination be "practical," as the law says it shall be. The civil service commission have performed their duty in this matter judiciously. That part of the examination which is intended to test the general fitness of applicants will not greatly tax the mental resources of any one possessing a common school education, unless expert services are required. The standard set is low rather than high. Sir G. O. Trevelyan says that the opening of the English civil and military services to competition, in its influence upon national education, was equivalent to a hundred thousand scholarships and exhibitions of the most valuable kind. Whatever may be the influence of the system of federal examinations upon the education of the American people, there cannot be two opinions as to the effect of that system upon the national character. It is needless to point out that a public contest of merit, into which any one may enter without fear or solicitation, induces high endeavor, and conserves manhood. On the other hand, it is equally patent that where offices go by favor, thrift follows fawning. Women seeking an honest career are reduced to importuning, mayhap subjected to insult; young men are transformed into mendicants and sycophants; and the position of all applicants does not differ materially from that of the Elizabethan courtier, whose ignominy Spenser, in travail of spirit, has described so vividly : —

> "Full little knowest thou, that hast not tride,
> What hell it is in suing long to bide :
> To loose good days, that might be better spent;
> To waste long nights in pensive discontent;

> To speed to-day, to be put back to-morrow;
> To feed on hope, to pine with feare and sorrow;
> To fret thy soul with crosses and with cares;
> To eate thy heart through comfortlesse dispaires;
> To fawne, to crouche, to wait, to ride, to ronne,
> To spend, to give, to want, to be undonne."

VII.

"This is the civil service that he [Jefferson] taught us, sir, — 'Is the man honest? Is he capable?' These were the only requirements. If, then, he is a man who is deserving, his employer should be the sole judge of it. When I make application for admission as an employee in one of the departments here, the head of the department is the man to inquire into my qualifications and honesty."[1]

That a representative of Tammany Hall should arise in the national Congress and gravely inveigh against the merit system on the ground that it does not embody the Jeffersonian requirements of honesty and capacity, is a spectacle calculated to excite pensive reflections upon the decadence of American humor.

---

[1] General Spinola, *Proceedings of the House of Representatives*, December 19, 1888.

That "ancient and powerful organization" might have informed itself that the Pendleton Act does not prevent the "head of a department" from looking into "the qualifications and honesty" of an applicant. The appointive power is not transferred by that measure. No one pretends that the secretary of a great department has the time personally to test the fitness, by examination or otherwise, of those applying for the numerous clerkships under his control. Under any system this duty must be delegated. The civil service commission is a convenience, simply, and is created as a guarantee of fair play. It does not appoint; it merely certifies to the result of the public competitive examinations held under its auspices. Its functions are ministerial, and its inquiries may be treated as preliminary. It is true that the head of the department cannot go outside the list of eligibles in making appointments; but it is true also that the whole public is invited to the competition, and thus has the opportunity to range itself within those lists.

If heads of departments, or rather chiefs of bureaus, ought to choose their own subordinates, then the objector quoted above has furnished an excellent reason why the spoils system, which he advocates, should be abolished. An unwritten law governing that system robs the chief of bureau of all discretion in the matter of appointments. Congressmen dictate to him whom he shall employ.

The questions: Is the applicant honest? Is he capable? are not controlling. Practically, the chief is precluded from discriminating inquiry; he must take what the Congressman sets before him. Nor is this all. He cannot discharge an unruly or inefficient employee without endangering his own head. Numerous instances might be quoted to show that clerks who have been dismissed by the chief for the good of the service have been restored by him under the pains and penalties of congressional insistence.

A system which permits outsiders thus to interfere in the conduct of the departments, and which transforms the civil service into a bankrupt court for the liquidation of political debt, can hardly be extolled as promotive of good administration. Much less are its defenders in a position to assail the merit system, which would appoint a chief of bureau by promotion, and which would secure to him such independence and discretion as are necessary to the proper performance of his duties.

VIII.

"The duties of all public officers are, or at least admit of being made, so plain and simple that men of intelligence may readily qualify themselves for their performance; and I cannot but believe that more is lost by the long continuance of men in office than is generally to be gained by their experience. I submit, therefore, to your consideration whether the efficiency of the government would not be promoted, and official industry and integrity better secured, by a general extension of the law which limits appointments to four years." [1]

President Jackson himself furnishes the best commentary upon his own text. Without waiting for Congress to act upon his recommendation to extend the four-year law, he immedi-

---

[1] Andrew Jackson's first annual message to Congress, December 8, 1829.

ately put his theory into practice by making removals wholesale, thus inaugurating the spoils system as we now know it. The effect was not at all what the public had been led to expect by the words of the annual message. Webster said, in a speech,[1] that during the first three years of the new administration (1829-32) more nominations had been " rejected [by the Senate] on the ground of unfitness than in all the preceding years of the government; and those nominations, you know, sir, could not have been rejected but by votes of the President's own friends." Nor did those persons who succeeded in passing the ordeal of senatorial confirmation give character to the service. The good name of the country was scandalized by great frauds. The loss which occurred in the handling of government funds during the eight years of Jackson's rule averaged $7.52 per thousand, an increase of $3.13 over that of his predecessor, John Quincy Adams. During the administration of Van Buren, — that perfect exponent of the spoils system and *protégé* of Jackson, — the deficits reached the great sum of

[1] Delivered at Worcester, Mass., October 12, 1832.

$11.72 per thousand, the high-water mark of inefficiency and corruption in the official history of the United States. This marked deterioration of the public service may be easily explained. Incumbents had been removed for political reasons, and not for purposes of administrative reform. Little wonder, then, that President Jackson should advocate the vacation of office by law, and thus save himself and his successors the odium of those evils which follow in the train of an arbitrary and indiscriminate proscription of place-holders.

IX.

"Rotation in office, change, is an absolute necessity. Our whole system abhors perpetuity. Rotation and change, the frequent examination of the servant's accounts, and the frequent removal of the servant himself, is an essential element to secure the perpetuity of free institutions." [1]

An examination of the servant's accounts should not wait upon removal, and the servant himself should not be removed unless there is

[1] Senator Williams, *Cong. Rec.*, vol. xiv. Part I. p. 505.

cause for it. "Change for the sake of change" is unsound as a political principle and impracticable as a business method. It would wreck any government or railroad that adopted it. In essence it is a pseudo-socialism. The theory that the citizen owes a duty to the state is supplanted by the doctrine that the state owes a place to the citizen; that government is a device for the support of its subjects; and that every man should be maintained in some mysterious and circuitous manner by every other man. This opens an alluring vista of possibilities. If every one "has a right to an office;" if incumbents should be removed simply because they have been in "long enough;" if official life is a "merry-go-round," it follows duly that rotation must successively induct into place every adult in the United States, for a period of time to be ascertained only by a nice calculation in the rule of three. Should it be objected that rotation is not rotatory, — that is, that it does not include all, — then the doctrine lacks even the apology of a common benefit, and becomes merely an alimentary provision for a few hungry office-seekers. As such it will not commend itself to the popular judgment. The people are not interested in the fortunes of itinerant place-hunters. They are interested, however, in having the business of the government — that is, the business of themselves — well done. But to refuse to recognize merit by promotion; to remove all officers, the faithful and the unfaithful, the efficient and the inefficient, the honest and the dishonest, indifferently, is to put a premium upon sloth, bungling, and peculation. In these days of sharp competition, commercial houses do not conduct their business so, and would not if they could. To employ a man with scant regard to his fitness, and to discharge him despite his skill, trustworthiness, and experience, would be to court ruin and to build up rival concerns. But it may be urged that the government is a monopoly, and can afford to ignore the economies; that the American people are rich, dislike cheese-paring, and are fond of "munificent public expenditure." Is the art of administration beneath the dignity of an intelligent people? It should be their pride. The United States is the most extravagant of civilized governments. What it wastes would enrich any third-class power. States and municipalities are groaning under debts recklessly incurred. In some cases, where the burdens have been too heavy to be borne, or where the public conscience has been weak, repudiation has left its indelible stain. Princely domains have been voted to railroads by federal and state legislatures. Tens of millions of dollars have been sunk in the improvement of unused water-ways, in half-finished canals, and in badly made roads. The enormous fees and salaries paid in many States to county officers have been a prolific source of office jobbery and of corrupt elections, and, it may be remarked in passing, afford a field for civil service reform which as yet is scarcely explored. As to municipal government, its name is a byword and a hissing. Valuable franchises, which ought to yield a permanent public revenue, have been, and are being, constantly given away to corporations. Insecure public buildings, defective sewage systems, illy paved and illy lighted streets, leaky aqueducts, and impure water supplies commemorate in almost every city the carelessness of a free people and the unfitness of their servants. A computation of the cost of government in this country, made by some careful statistician, would be an interesting object lesson to the taxpayer. That much-exploited individual is awakening at last to the fact that something is wrong. He is beginning to doubt whether the "hustler" or the "worker" is the ideal administrative officer. To choose a city civil engineer because he is a "good fellow," and to appoint an architect of federal buildings because he is a cousin of the President's step-aunt, no longer seems to him to be a wholly rational proceeding. The idea that every American is qualified, without previous training or experience, to fill any office has proved to be an expensive delusion. The most incompetent men in the civil service of the United States are those who are appointed for short terms. About 3,500 of the higher-grade officers are so selected by the President and the Senate, but the business of the places themselves is in the hands of subordinates, upon whom the superior is helplessly dependent. As a rule, the presidential postmaster knows nothing of the workings of his office. Although he is the highest in rank, he becomes, by force of circumstances, the pupil of the lowest. He learns his duties at the expense of the government, and, as often as not, is removed at the very time he begins to be serviceable. The same is also true of other officers, including the members of the cabinet. The case of the last named, however, is exceptional. These officials are quasi-legislative, as well as administrative. As the political advisers of the President, and indirectly of Congress, and as the exponents of a party or national policy, they should be removable at pleasure. If the effect of this commingling of duties is not always salutary, it furnishes sometimes an agreeable diversion to the disinterested spectator. The facility with which members of the cabinet are shifted from one department to another, during the same administration, indicates either great versatility in the American administrative officer, or (more probably) a profound and impartial ignorance that is not less impressive. At the best, the technical knowledge possessed by the heads of departments is superficial, and the rapidity of cabinet changes merely emphasizes the need for experienced subordinates. Indeed, experience, of which duration in office is generally the measure, is absolutely indispensable.

But the advocates of rotation cite the many excellences of the civil administration of the United States as proof of their theory. It disproves it. Parties have not alternated in the control of the government every four years, as the Constitution permits. They have had extended leases of power, and, while many changes have been made in the *personnel* of the service, the body of the employees have been retained long enough to enable them to become familiar with their duties, and to administer their offices with economy and dispatch. Mr. Eaton, the American encyclopædist of civil service reform, writing in 1884, said that "the average periods of service in the lower offices, of late, at least, have been two or three times four years, and have been the longest where administration has been best and politics least partisan and corrupt. The average time of service of the more than 42,000 postmasters, whose terms are not fixed by law, has probably been about ten years, at least, if we exclude post-offices established within that period."[1]

---

[1] *Lalor's Cyclopædia*, vol. iii. p. 904.

Here, then, we are face to face with the difficulty (before stated) which confronted England, namely: to obtain good government, either the spoils system must be abolished, or some one party must be continued in power indefinitely. "Rotation" is already discredited in business communities. It exists in theory only because it is infrequent in practice. A few successive trials of it will be a liberal education to all persons concerned.

But it is urged, with some patriotic fervor, that "our system abhors perpetuity;" that rotation is a fundamental principle of democracy; and that it is essential to the permanence of our institutions.

Whether a government, established for the common benefit of the whole people, "abhors" the "perpetuity" of anything that helps to secure that end is a question which perhaps even the wayfaring man might answer, without invoking the aid of the casuist.

The government of the United States was formed as a protest against tyranny; that is, against the rule of unfit and irresponsible men. The fitness and responsibility of rulers were among the germinal ideas of the Constitution. Hereditary kingships and hereditary houses of legislation were abolished by that instrument. Merit, and not accident of birth, was to be the test of official preferment. Civil service reform embodies this ideal. It says that those officers of the executive department whose duties, being purely administrative and not legislative, are the same, whatever party is in power, shall be appointed from the whole people, solely on account of fitness; that they shall not be secured in place for any fixed term, be it short or long; and that their tenure shall depend upon their good behavior and efficiency. Obviously, this tenure, which means the instant decapitation of the unfit servant, is a very different thing from life tenure, which means a vested interest in office.

Several facts prove conclusively that the founders of the republic took this view of the matter. In the first place, they fixed the term of no officer in the executive department except that of the President and the Vice-President. Secondly, they provided by express words in the Constitution that the judges of the Supreme

Court and the inferior courts should hold their offices during good behavior. Thirdly, they applied this system to the civil administration at the very beginning of the government. The allegation, then, that a tenure of this character, which was an established usage for forty years, is radical, revolutionary, and subversive of "our system" may be leniently ascribed to the inaccurate tendencies of the florid and rhetorical mind.

Strange as it may appear to earnest but misguided vociferants, there has been no statutory change in the tenure of the great majority of inferior officers in the civil branch of the executive department. Custom, it is true, has wrought a decided change in that it has substituted a tenure of favoritism and partisanship; but no legal barrier to continuous service has been erected. An appointee under the spoils system may grow gray in the government service, provided always that he can gain and retain the influence of some potent politician. Probably the advocates of rotation will not greatly object to this, if the incumbent belongs to "their side." Indeed, it is painful, as a commentary upon the perishable nature of political convictions, to observe how speedily the party in power becomes reconciled to that perpetuity in office which erstwhile was so abhorrent. It leaves it to the party which is out of power — those who are unbidden to the feast — to become "aghast" at the enormity of the thing. Did not the dominant party thus acquiesce periodically in a stable holding, the doctrine of rotation would have vanished in disgrace long since.

As far back as 1835, Mr. Calhoun pointed out the distinction which is necessary to a proper understanding of the rotation theory. In advocating the repeal of the four-year law, with the ablest men of the Senate, including Webster, Clay, Benton, and others, he said : —

"I will not undertake to inquire now whether the principle of rotation, as applied to the ordinary ministerial officers of a government, may not be favorable to popular and free institutions, when such officers are chosen by the people themselves. It certainly would have a tendency to cause those who desire office, when the choice is in the people, to seek their favor ; but certain it is, that in a Government where the Chief Magistrate has the filling of vacancies, instead of the people, there will be an opposite tendency, — to court the favor of him who has the disposal of offices, — and this for the very reason that when the choice is in the people their favor is courted. If the latter has a popular tendency, it is no less certain that the former must have a contrary one." [1]

If this reasoning suggests to zealous advocates of rotation the propriety of making the ministerial offices of the executive department elective, and thereby amenable to the people, another quotation — one from the publicist, John Stuart Mill — may be permitted: —

"A most important principle of good government in a popular constitution is that no executive functionaries should be appointed by popular election, neither by the votes of the people themselves nor by those of their representatives. The entire business of government is skilled employment; the qualifications for the discharge of it are of that special and professional kind which cannot be properly judged of except by persons who have themselves some share of those qualifications, or some practical experience of them. The business of finding the fittest

---

[1] *Works*, vol. ii. pp. 445, 446.

persons to fill public employment — not merely selecting the best who offer, but looking out for the absolutely best, and taking note of all fit persons who are met with, that they may be found when wanted — is very laborious, and requires a delicate as well as highly conscientious discernment; and as there is no public duty which is in general so badly performed, so there is none for which it is of greater importance to enforce the utmost practicable amount of personal responsibility, by imposing it as a special obligation on high functionaries in the several departments. All subordinate public officers who are not appointed by some mode of public competition should be selected on the direct responsibility of the minister under whom they serve."[1]

If, to suppose a case, the 57,000 postmasters in the United States were elected by the people, what would be the efficiency of the Post-Office Department? Instead of a coördinated whole, regulated by and responsible to a single head, there would be a multitude of independent units — a debating society. The Postmaster-General, denuded of all authority, would be a figure-head, an adviser, not a commander. Even if the

[1] *Rep. Gov.*, pp. 268, 269.

power of removal were secured to him, he could not exercise it without affronting the judgment of the particular constituency that elected the displaced officer. Appeals from his decisions to the electoral bodies would be frequent, and would result in endless confusion. Under such circumstances an administrative system would be impossible. Blame for maladministration could not be fixed, and responsibility is vital to good government. "As a general rule, every executive function, whether superior or subordinate, should be the appointed duty of some given individual. It should be apparent to all the world who did everything, and through whose default anything was left undone. Responsibility is null when nobody knows who is responsible; nor, even when real, can it be divided without being weakened." [1]

Municipalities are beginning to lay this lesson to heart. Government by boards of aldermen and by councils, whose members are answerable, not to the whole city, but to separate districts, is a famous contrivance for ill doing and not doing. For these joint feasors there is no common

[1] *Rep. Gov.*, p. 262.

court. But if authority were fused, it would be easier to mete out punishment. A mayor elected by the whole community, and endowed with the power of appointing boards of public works, would receive the full meed of praise or blame. Charged with malfeasance, he could not, Adam-like, lay it on another. Solely responsible, he would present a conspicuous figure for public sacrifice. Complexity is the weakness of popular government; simplicity is its genius. The mass move slowly, and it is the height of unwisdom to distract their attention from one to many by diffusing responsibility. This reasoning applies to all administrative government, whether local or national. It tells strongly against the four-year law, which divides between the Président and the Senate the responsibility of appointing the higher administrative officers of the United States. This law, which is the exemplar of rotation, increases the power of the President by compelling a new appointment every four years. It also decreases his responsibility. To use the words of Webster, "the law itself vacates the office, and gives the means of rewarding a friend without the exercise of the power of removal at all."[1] If the friend thus appointed is incompetent, unfaithful, or dishonest, the President can plead, in extenuation, that the Senate coöperated with him in the selection of the officer. But the Senators themselves escape individual censure, because all confirmations occur in secret session. It was said in defense of this cumbrous method of choice that the Senate, in acting upon a nomination by the President, would look solely to the fitness of the candidate, and that "its advice and consent" would be disinterested. Experience refutes this. In many instances, nominations are ratified, not because the nominees are fit, but because their names have been suggested by the very Senators who pass upon them. In other instances, the power of "senatorial courtesy" is invoked, and nominations are rejected because the nominees are personally objectionable to the Senators of some particular State. Division of responsibility here means division of spoil.

The first four-year law (passed in 1820) was

[1] *The Appointing and Removing Power*, U. S. Senate, February 16, 1835.

the herald of the patronage system. "The bill was retroactive, and it made official terms expire upon the eve of the presidential election." It was drawn by Mr. Crawford, who expected to be, and was, a candidate for the presidency in 1824.

"The avowed reason, or rather the apology, for the new policy was that it would remove unworthy officers; the speciousness of which appears in the facts that the tenures of all in office, worthy and unworthy alike, were, without inquiry, severed absolutely; and nothing but official pleasure was to protect the most meritorious in the future. There was no showing of delinquencies; no charge that the President could not or would not remove unworthy officials; not a word of discussion, not a record of votes, on this revolutionary bill!"[1]

In the lapse of time the provisions of the bill were extended. With the downfall of the congressional caucus the initiative in the nomination of Presidents passed to the country at large. Thus it happened that "workers" were needed in every quarter to advance the interests of can-

[1] D. B. Eaton. *Labor's Cyclopædia*, vol. iii. p. 900.

didates, and these men must be paid. But how? To abolish tenure on good behavior and to legislate incumbents out of office every four years was an easy and admirable expedient. This was done in the case of postmasters drawing a salary of a thousand dollars per annum, or more, and of some others, and the law now covers nearly all the high-salaried officials on the civil list. The Pendleton Act affects only their subordinates; and our administrative system to-day presents the anomaly of filling certain inferior offices by the test of merit, and of jobbing out the superior offices as political rewards. If the civil service act is to be honestly enforced, the four-year law must be repealed. Postmasters, collectors, heads of divisions, and bureaus, who are themselves the creatures of favoritism, and who are daily beset by "workers" clamoring for office, cannot be expected to look kindly upon a law which is a reproach to their own existence, and which denies to them the power to pay the men who have made them what they are. There is another consideration: the highest positions demand the largest capacity and the longest experience. But the four-year law makes the supply smallest where the demand is greatest. Again, to subject subordinates to ignorant and incapable superiors is to demoralize the service. The lower should look upward, not the higher downward.

It may be admitted that there is a deep-rooted popular objection to the repeal of the four-year law, and the reason is plain. Federal offices have been used so long as party spoils, and have been so much the subject of contention, that the people have come to regard them as not less important than legislative offices, and to look with as grave distrust upon long tenure in the one as in the other. This mistake is not unnatural. These offices are filled by prominent politicians, who, by reason of their election work, have become obnoxious to many of the community. To keep such factious persons in place indefinitely seems to the public the greatest kind of an evil. But the repeal of the four-year law will not perpetuate this evil; it will abolish it. It will bring into office a different class of men, who will be little in the public eye, and whose energies will be devoted to the public, and not to party interests.

So much for the doctrine of rotation, seriously and tenderly considered. Stripped of its pretentious and misleading verbiage, it means, not the purification of the civil service, but the displacement of one horde of office-seekers by another. It is the cry of foray, not the watchword of reform. It is an excuse, not a reason. It is the sign and symbol of a predatory raid, the rallying banner of landless resolutes enlisted to an enterprise that hath a stomach in it. Looked at in any way, rotation is a perpetually recurring menace to the stability of our government. It is the prop of a falling party, and the instrument of fraud. It is a constant temptation to politicians to use public salaries as a fund with which to pay private debts, thus compelling the people to furnish the means for their own corruption and to defeat their own will. It wrecks the lives of tens of thousands of young men by offering, as a bait to cupidity, high wages which outbid the market. It makes idle expectants of the industrious, starves the few it feeds, and lures the mass to vagrancy. It subverts the true ideal of office, transforming public servants into private henchmen, and partisans into camp followers. It degrades skilled labor, and makes the government an almshouse. It breeds parasites, markets citizenship, and suborns public opinion. To sum up, it makes of administration a chaos, of politics a trade, and of principle an interest. Rotation is not an "essential element to secure the perpetuity of free institutions."

www.ingramcontent.com/pod-product-compliance
Lightning Source LLC
Chambersburg PA
CBHW031833230426
43669CB00009B/1332